SHOTGUNS AND CARTRIDGES

An automatic loading machine which checks its own operations continuously for correct powder volume, presence of wads and position of the total wad column, and stops in the event of any error (Westley Richards)

Shotguns and Cartridges

GOUGH THOMAS

(G. T. GARWOOD, M.SC., F.I.C.E., F.I.E.E.
GUN EDITOR, THE SHOOTING TIMES)

New and enlarged edition
with line illustrations by the author

ADAM & CHARLES BLACK
LONDON

First published 1963 by Electrical Press Ltd.,
Maidenhead, Berks

This revised and enlarged edition
published 1970, reprinted 1972
by A. & C. Black Ltd.,
4, 5 and 6, Soho Square, London W1V 6AD

ISBN 0 7136 1139 1

Printed in Great Britain by
Bristol Typesetting Co., Ltd.
Barton Manor, St. Philips, Bristol

CONTENTS

CHAPTER		PAGE
	Preface to the Second Edition	9
	Introduction	11
1.	Historical Background	13
2.	Modern Guns	18
3.	Choice of a Gun (Type)	30
4.	Choice of a Gun (Performance)	39
5.	Patterns	52
6.	Choke	60
7.	Cartridges	70
8.	Home-Loading and Reloading	82
9.	Weight and Recoil	92
10.	Clay Pigeon Guns	97
11.	Magnum Guns	102
12.	Balance	105
13.	Stocks and Fitting	113
14.	Miscellanea	119
	Appendix	129
	Index	133

PLATES

An automatic loading machine	Frontispiece
	FACING PAGE
The hammer gun at the peak of its development—A typical Anson & Deeley gun	14
An inexpensive Spanish gun—The French Darne sliding breech gun	15
The trigger plate mechanism of a Perazzi gun—The Webley-Greener Martini action G.P. gun	32
A typical London-pattern sidelock gun—The Holland & Holland self-opening mechanism	33
A typical American pump gun—An American bolt action repeater	48
The F. N. Browning short-recoil automatic—The F. N. Browning long-recoil automatic—A typical American gas-operated automatic shotgun	49
Barrel boring—Machined body of boxlock gun	64
A collet-type adjustable choke—A typical modern plastic wad—The Winchester " Winchoke "	65
A modern Eley cartridge—The Winchester compression-formed cartridge	80
A shot charge in flight—X-rayed cartridges—Testing Eley cartridges	81
A popular loading machine—A beam balance—The Westley Richards single trigger	96
An F. N. Browning over-and-under trap gun—An S.K.B. over-and-under trap gun	97

A comb raised to cure low shooting—The Singlepoint sight 112

The French Darne gun in the open position—A modern breech-loading punt gun 113

FIGURES

PAGE

1. Early Tudor matchlock 14
2. Anson & Deeley action 20
3. A conventional sidelock 21
4. The Southgate ejector 23
5. Release trigger 25
6. Working principle of a long-recoil automatic 26
7. Working principle of a short-recoil automatic 27
8. Effective ranges 47
9. 40-yard pattern, improved cylinder 56
10. 40-yard pattern, full choke 56
11. 20-yard pattern, improved cylinder 57
12. 20-yard pattern, full choke 57
13. 80-yard pattern, fully choked automatic 63
14. Types of choke 64
15. Spread of small and large bores 65
16. Aiming target for demonstrating spread 67
17. The Cutts compensator 68
18. Cold welding of shot pellets 74
19. Effect of progressive powders 75
20. High-velocity and normal cartridges compared 78
21. The Wanda cartridge 79
22. The principle of a muzzle-brake 93
23. Composite gun movement resolved into components 106
24. Measuring balance 109
25. Equivalent distribution of weight 110
26. The measurements of a gun-stock 114

27. 12-bore rifled slug 121
28. Mirage created by warm air layer 124
Current nitro-proof marks 130
Current foreign nitro-proof marks 131

TABLES

PAGE

1. Minimum patterns 42
2. Percentage patterns for all borings at all ranges 43 & 62
3. Striking energy for individual pellets 43
4. Pellets in game charges 49
5. Definitions of choke 61
6. Diameter of spread 62
7. Black powder loads 86
8. Recommended loads for paper tube cartridges 88
9. Recommended loads for plastic tube cartridges 89
10. Balance data—best guns 111
11. Balance data—other guns 111
12. Punt gun sizes and loads 127

PREFACE TO THE SECOND EDITION

THE FIRST edition of this book was criticised as being too short. It was, indeed, written under severe limitation as to space. In the present edition that limitation has been substantially relaxed and I have taken advantage of the opportunity to add much new material, including three completely new chapters, and to bring the book thoroughly up to date.

In its present form it will, I hope, provide the practical but enquiring sportsman with all he needs for an adequate understanding of modern shotguns and their ammunition. At the same time, several of the matters now briefly dealt with, more especially as concerning the choice, testing and appraisal of guns, are elaborated in my *Gough Thomas's Gun Book*. The two books, indeed, are largely complementary—a fact that will, I hope, excuse the several references to the latter herein.

I gratefully acknowledge the help and guidance I have received in the choice of matter for the present edition from the extensive correspondence I have conducted over the past decade with readers of the *Shooting Times & Country Magazine*, which I have had the privilege of serving in the capacity of Gun Editor.

In conclusion, I have to thank the proprietors for permission to make use of matter originally published in that journal; Imperial Metal Industries Limited for permission to reproduce Tables 2, 3, 4 and 6 from their admirable publication "The Shooter's Year Book" (57th edn.), as well as for other data and co-operation generously afforded by Mr. J. W. Huskins on their behalf. I also have to thank the following firms and others who kindly supplied illustrations, namely, Imperial Metal Industries Ltd., Messrs. James Purdey & Sons Ltd., Westley Richards & Co.

Ltd., Webley & Scott Ltd., Gallyon & Sons Ltd., Anglo Spanish Imports, Etablissements Darne, L. LePersonne & Co. Ltd., Millard Bros., O. F. Mossberg & Sons, The Remington Arms Co., Thomas Bland & Sons, B.S.A. Guns Ltd., Leslie Hewitt Ltd., Holland & Holland Ltd., the Lyman Gun Sight Corporation, Olin (Winchester-Western Division), Polychoke Co., Singlepoint (G.B.) Ltd., The Worshipful Company of Gunmakers and the Proof Master and Guardians of the Birmingham Proof House. My cordial thanks are also due to Joan Clifford for generously undertaking the duties of amanuensis and critic.

INTRODUCTION

I ALWAYS feel that it is a pity for a shooting man to be too keen on guns—it seems to be subordinating a major to a minor interest. There is so much more in shooting than the mere weapons of the chase. In many ways it takes a man back, body and spirit, to the places where he belongs, and gives him back so many of the things of which modern commercial civilisation has deprived him. Air, freedom and exercise; wild nature; the good companionship of dogs and men; and the eternally thrilling pursuit of a wild quarry destined for wholesome food, are surely its main sources of delight.

And yet there is a very special relation between a man and his gun—an atavistic relation with its roots deep in pre-history, when the primitive man's personal weapon, so often his only effective defence and food-provider, was nearly as precious to him as one of his own limbs. Small wonder that instinct should invest the modern man's gun with some faint aura of this quality, enhanced, as it may well be, by his recognising it as an old friend, the indispensable companion of some of his best days and the agent of some of his best-remembered successes.

And so, within their love of shooting, many men find room to love a gun. I count myself as being of their company; and it is for such as these that I have written this book, knowing, as my work for the *Shooting Times* has taught me, the sort of things on which they and their sons most often seek further knowledge and guidance. I have not written for the specialist, amateur or professional, in any branch of gun-knowledge or practice. Rather, I write as an ordinary shooter, whose qualifications are a lifelong interest in guns and shooting, a long experience, and a professional training which throws light on some aspects of the subject.

In planning my coverage, I have adopted, as being more appropriate to the times, a less insular approach than that of most previous British writers in this field. Indeed, there has never been a time when such an approach was justified in a general work.

CHAPTER ONE

HISTORICAL BACKGROUND

To UNDERSTAND how modern guns came about, and to form certain judgments about them, it is necessary to consider something of their history.

In this country, the use of firearms for taking feathered and ground game may be conveniently dated from the end of the Wars of the Roses in 1485, during which the smooth-bore matchlock (Fig. 1) was perfected. This was a gun in which the charge was ignited by a smouldering cord or " match " worked by a simple trigger mechanism.

The troubled times had no doubt acquainted many humble folk with the use of this crude but exciting new weapon, and had shown them that it could be more fruitfully employed in augmenting food supplies than in killing men. A number of factors were thus brought into combination which were destined to bring about great social changes. On the one hand, there was the gun itself, an effective arm against sitting targets; and on the other there were seemingly inexhaustible stocks of game, wildfowl and other edible birds against which it could be successfully employed. When to these were added the endemic winter food shortages that existed among the poorer classes, and the fact that, over the greater part of the country, fowling was lawful and free to any man who could possess himself of the means to practise it, the great upsurge that took place in shooting can be seen to have been inevitable. Attempts to check it by legislation, inspired by legitimate fears for our national supremacy in the use of the longbow, and no doubt with some thought for the fillip which the gun had given to deer-poaching—not to mention robbery with violence—were totally unavailing. In the absence of effective enforcement, nothing could deter the rustic population from using this new means for stocking their scanty larders. Besides, we may be sure that the shooting peasantry of early Tudor days thoroughly enjoyed their pot-hunting; for although the matchlock was incapable of wing shooting, it offered all the thrills of stalking. And so, as Shakespeare indicates, its popularity spread upwards to the new, well-fed, mercantile classes of the Elizabethan era.

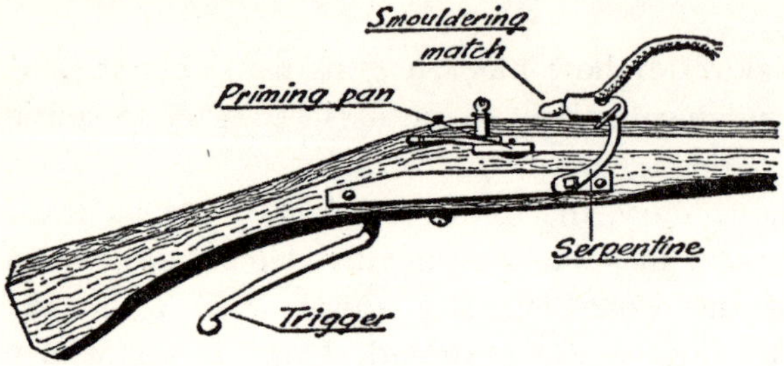

Fig. 1. Early Tudor Matchlock. This exciting new weapon—or so it must have appeared to a peasant of the period—notably improved the standard of his winter living by enabling him to take toll of the great numbers of wildfowl that flocked the undrained meres of fifteenth-century England—not to mention, less lawfully, the herds of wild deer that roamed royal chase and lordly domain.

But the nobility and privileged classes remained almost wholly outside this movement: for their sporting, they continued to rely on horse, hound and hawk, whereby the nascent gun trade of this country languished for lack of aristocratic and wealthy patronage.

Not so on the Continent, where the upper classes appear to have been less conservative. There the matchlock was freely used, both as an adjunct to the conventional chase and as a hunting weapon in its own right. From its early days it had been rifled, and had thereby gained greatly in power and precision, so that it could be used effectively against deer and wild boar up to about 200 yards. The beautifully made and ornamented specimens to be seen in our museums provide abundant evidence of its eager adoption by the Continental aristocracy, whose patronage and encouragement soon established flourishing *ateliers*

The hammer gun at the peak of its development, with rebounding locks, small, neat hammers entirely below the line of sight when cocked, top-lever, snap-action, Purdey double bolt, Greener cross-bolt and Purdey side-clips

A typical Birmingham-made Anson & Deeley gun (see also fig. 2). This simple and durable kind of weapon, costing about £10 before World War I, and sold in very large numbers, chiefly sustained the high reputation of English guns in the remoter parts of the world

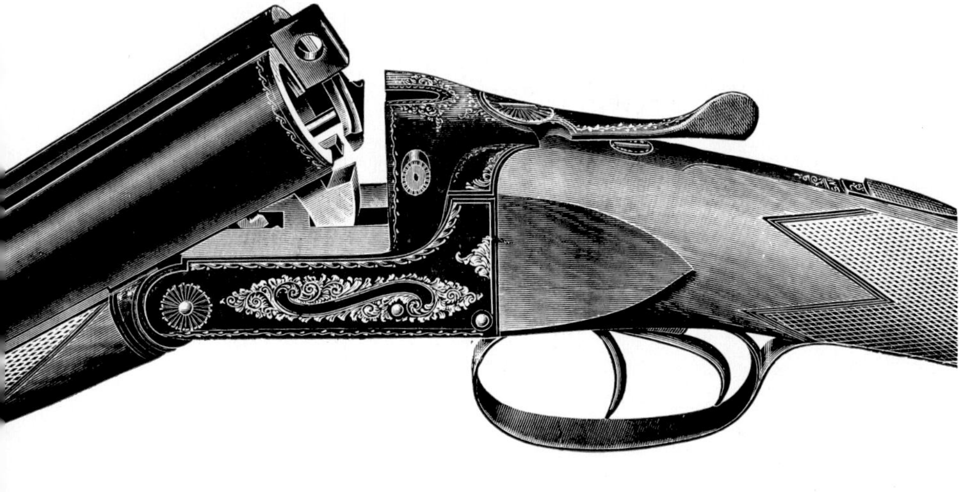

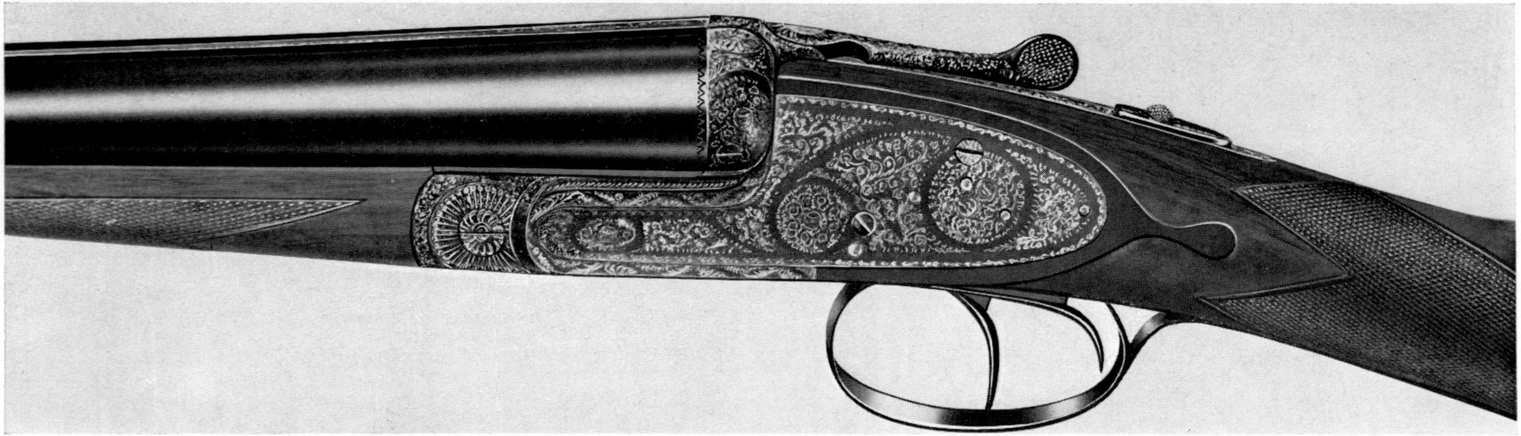

Above: An inexpensive Spanish gun (AYA No. 1). Faithfully modelled on best quality English guns, it captures much of their beauty and elegance

Below: The French Darne sliding breech gun—strong, light, simple and highly elegant in the better grades. See also the plate facing page 113

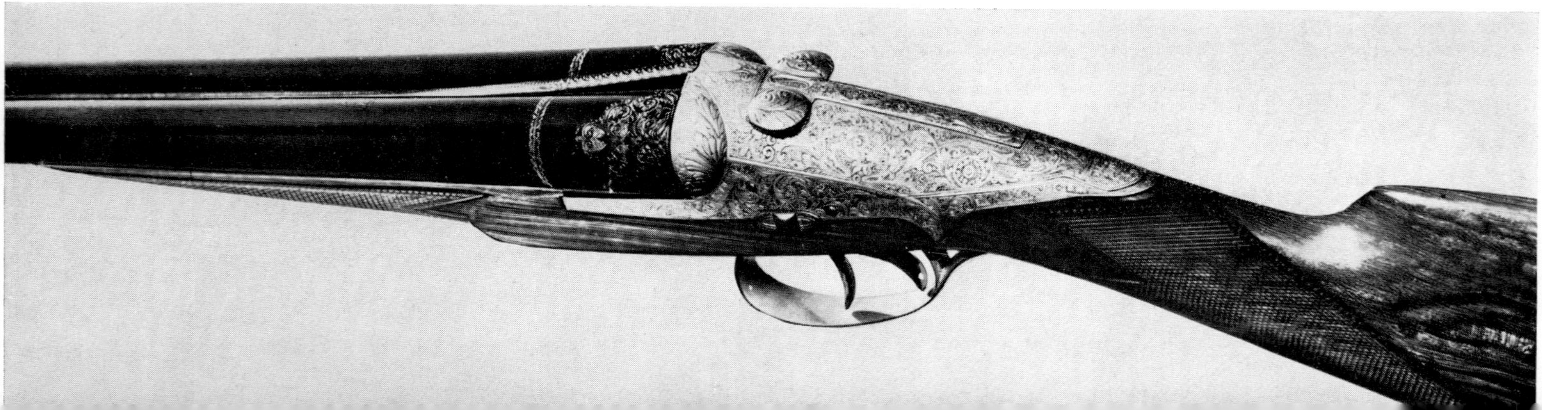

for the manufacture of high-class sporting arms in most of the centres that remain famous to this day—St. Etienne, Liège, and Brescia among others.

A new impetus was given to the sport of shooting and to the Continental arms industry by the development of the wheel-lock in Nuremburg around 1520. This invention, with what must have seemed to be its well-nigh miraculous quality of giving instant fire, enabled a gun for the first time to be loaded and kept in a state of constant readiness and instantly discharged by the touch of a trigger. It was a weapon of considerable complexity, the art of making which, though highly cultivated abroad, hardly spread across the Channel. The relatively few specimens seen in this country were invariably importations, procured by wealthy enthusiasts, among whom that royal gun-lover, Henry VIII, stands pre-eminent.

Shooting becomes fashionable

The origin of the next great invention—the "pecking-hen" flintlock—is obscure, but by 1625 a typically English form had been developed. It was, however, slow in action, and did little or nothing to extend the stalking tactics or social background of shooting. But with the return of Charles II from his exile in France in 1660, there was a big change, for he brought with him in his entourage many who had learnt the new French sport of shooting birds on the wing, which French improvements in the flintlock had rendered possible. The sport quickly became fashionable, and stimulated our home gun trade into meeting the demand for the new, improved fowling pieces. From that time onward, shooting became what it has been ever since—one of our great national sports, the love of which is rooted in all classes.

By the end of another century, say by 1760, the best English gunmakers had more or less caught up the long start of their Continental rivals; and in the next half century, they succeeded in overtaking them. They did this, be it noted, not by any Heaven-ordained superiority, but by the sheer excellence of their guns—their shooting powers, their faultless workmanship and their severe elegance, in which, latterly, the pervasive influence of Beau Brummel on the taste of the period can be distinctly traced.

A sporting revolution

The overthrow of the perfected flintlock by the percussion muzzle-loader, to which we may attach the date of 1825, though a technical revolution, is of little significance to the present theme. It was the introduction of the pinfire breechloader by the Paris gunmaker, Lefaucheux, towards the middle of the century, that revolutionised, not only guns, but the whole sport and practice of shooting. The English gunmakers, still the world-leaders, threw themselves into the task of perfecting the new weapon with furious energy. Urged on by a large and wealthy clientele, who demanded weapons equal to the exacting requirements of driven game shooting and the making of enormous bags, and at the same time of the highest elegance, safety and lasting quality, they evolved our modern hammerless ejector. It was a weapon forged in a white heat of competitive ingenuity and cunning craftsmanship for which it would be hard to find a parallel. Small wonder that, after three-quarters of a century, it should have changed so little.

The American contribution

We pass now to America, where, throughout the nineteenth century, the imported English gun held pride of place. But by historical imperative the U.S.A. was destined to become the birthplace of the repeater. The Civil War had left an arms industry with a large surplus capacity for the production of arms, including repeating rifles, by modern methods. Around the fringe of the settled areas were immense stocks of game and wildfowl which were slaughtered without limit by market-gunners. There was therefore a large potential demand from a protected home market for a cheap repeating shotgun, as well as the means for satisfying it. In the circumstances, the ultimate production of such weapons was inevitable; and when they duly emerged towards the end of the century, they were favourably received by a people eager for whatever was new and ingenious and American. And so repeaters took root and flourished on American soil. But these highly mechanical weapons cannot be regarded simply as part of the continuing evolution of the sporting gun: they were a development *sui generis*—an offshoot of a war industry, the mark of which they bear to this day. Europe, with commendable discrimination, remained faithful to the conventional double-barrelled gun. Though repeaters have been on sale here for fully half a century, for a long time they made no material progress, and apparently it did not occur to Burrard even to mention them when he wrote his monumental work on the shotgun nearly forty years ago. But in recent years, the repeater has attracted many adherents among the younger shooters, and those who entered the sport through clay pigeon shooting.

The modern picture

The present position of the sporting gun in this country is possibly fairly reflected in two personal observations—that in over forty years' experience covering every type of shooting practised in and around the British Isles, I have never yet seen anything but conventional guns in use in regular shooting parties of which I have been a member; but I nevertheless noticed that, at a recent Game Fair, probably one in four of all the guns being used at the clay pigeon shooting competitions was a repeater.

CHAPTER TWO

MODERN GUNS

As a preliminary to considering the choice of a gun in the next chapter, we must survey the guns available to the modern shooter in this country. They are single and double guns of 4, 8, 10, 12, 16, 20, 28 and .410 bore, with the 12-bore greatly preponderating. The 4-bore is rare and obsolescent, production of the ammunition having recently ceased. It is a matter for conjecture how long it will be before the 8 and 10-bore follow it. For the rest, these guns fall into two broad divisions to which I have had some difficulty in assigning fair and proper descriptions.

The first division includes all guns made by the traditional methods of the gun trade—a trade, incidentally, which is not in its origins a branch of engineering, but is traceably descended from that of the mediaeval armourer. These guns are made to designs evolved in the field and based on fitness for purpose rather than on the exigencies of economical manufacture. The cheaper sort are made by fundamentally the same methods, but of less expensive materials and to simpler designs, and are put together by less highly-skilled and highly-paid craftsmen in far less time. Less time is also spent on general finish and on adjusting and regulating the mechanism, and perhaps no time at all on testing or regulating the shooting.

The other broad division comprises all guns made by modern machine-shop methods. They are made to designs evolved on the drawing board rather than in the field, with a view chiefly to mass production by machinery. The best of them, regarded as engineering products, are beautifully made, and are good value for money.

One is tempted to label these two broad divisions as hand-made or gunmakers' guns, and machine-made or engineers' guns. But that would be misleading, for the maker of the traditional type of weapon, even in its most costly form, uses machine-shop methods so far as possible to get down to the outside tolerances of action and barrels, and very rightly so; whilst the manufacturer of the allegedly machine-made kind is no doubt unable to avoid putting in a considerable amount of hand-work in finishing, assembly and adjustment, to an extent dependent on the type and quality of the weapon. So, to avoid unfair and misleading implications, I will take advantage of the fact that the newer kinds of guns are almost invariably repeaters to label my broad divisions conventional guns and repeaters respectively.

CONVENTIONAL GUNS

These are predominantly the double-barrelled, drop-down guns, which can be either side-by-side or over-and-under. The single-barrelled kind must also be included. Other candidates for inclusion are the French sliding-breech type pioneered by Darne and possibly the combination gun-rifle or *drilling* of Germany. The Darne is entitled to rank under this heading because it is a gunmaker's gun in large-scale production with a history as long as that of the conventional hammerless ejector—also because of its availability on the British market and its suitability for British sport. But because it hardly conforms to this last particular, I have excluded the *drilling*.

The outstanding features of the guns I have grouped in this main division are as follows.

DOUBLE-BARRELLED, SIDE-BY-SIDE. Five subdivisions of this category must be considered.

(a) *Hammer—non-ejector*. A strong and simple design. Old, high quality specimens can be very beautiful but, as found, are usually proved for black powder only, and unless and until re-proved, are unsuitable for use with modern smokeless ammunition. Prone to inadvertent discharge, irrespective of quality, by faulty manipulation; though many eminent sportsmen, including King George V, continued to prefer this type long after hammerless guns had come into general use. They are slower in action than hammerless guns.

(*b*) *Hammerless box-lock (ejector or non-ejector).* Usually, if English, made on the Anson & Deeley system—the simplest, most robust, best understood and most readily repaired and adjusted of all sporting guns. Except only for the hammerless sidelock, the least accident-prone. Made in all qualities, and easily the most thoroughly proved sporting gun in the world. The simple lockwork is accom-

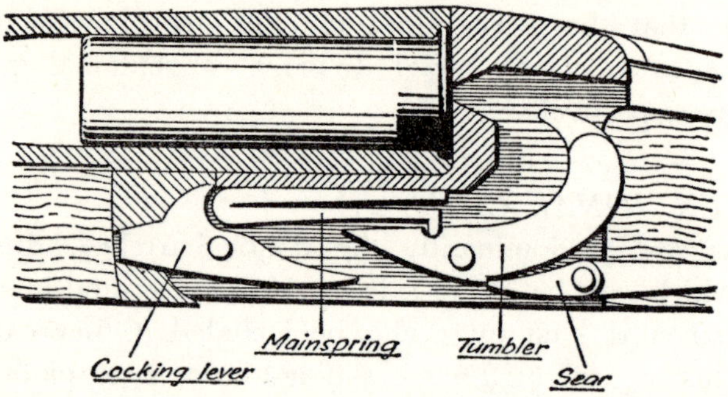

Fig. 2. Anson & Deeley Action. Introduced in 1875 by Westley Richards, this triumphant simplification is still the most widely used of all conventional gun actions. As shown, it is in the cocked position ready for firing. Pulling the trigger depresses the nose of the sear clear of the notch or " bent " in the tumbler, which is thereupon impelled by the mainspring to strike the cartridge. When the gun is opened after firing, the cocking lever, carried around by the fore-end, restores the tumbler to the position shown.
See also plate facing page 14.

modated in slots machined out of a solid action body. Some Continental box-locks, loosely described as " Anson & Deeley " are variants, and need individual appraisal. Balance and handling qualities, fair to very good. Normal weight of a 2½-inch, 12-bore with 28-inch barrels—6 lb. 6 oz. to 6 lb. 8 oz.

(*c*) *Hammerless sidelock (usually ejector).* The locks are mounted on detachable plates let into the side of the action and stock. They usually incorporate intercepting safety sears as a safeguard against the lock jarring off, as by a fall. A more elegant weapon than the box-lock—somewhat less simple and a good deal more costly, but usually better balanced and with superior trigger pulls. Everlasting in the best grades if well treated, but cheap versions need critical buying. Corresponding weight— 6 lb. 4 oz. to 6 lb. 6 oz. (See also below under *Ejectors, Single triggers and Self-opening actions.*)

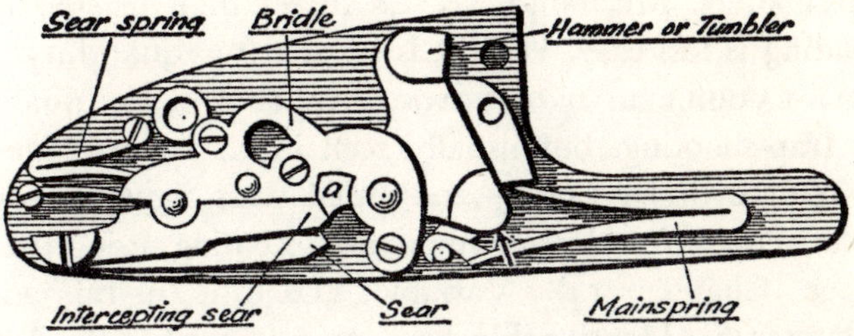

Fig. 3. A Conventional Sidelock. Here shown in the fired position. When the gun is opened, a see-saw lever (not shown) pivoted in the knuckle of the action and carried around by the fore-end, lifts the hammer or tumbler where shown by the arrow and restores it to the cocked position. Pulling the trigger depresses the nose of the sear and also that of the intercepting sear, thus allowing the hammer to fall; but if the sear alone is disengaged, as by a jar, the intercepting block *a*, which is part of the tumbler, is arrested by the nose of the intercepting sear, thus preventing the fall of the hammer.

(*d*) *Sliding breech* (*Darne*). Barrels are fixed in relation to stock; the gun is loaded by sliding back the standing breech. Strong, light, simple and highly elegant in the better grades. Light recoil. Balance and liveliness outstanding because of the rearward disposition of weight. Hand-detachable locks and ejectors in all models. Gun takes down into two parts only. Corresponding weight—6 lb. 2½ oz.

(*e*) *Trigger plate actions*. In these, the whole of the percussion mechanism is mounted on the trigger plate and is detachable therewith. Only British representative is the Dickson "round action", normally a side-by-side. An outstanding Continental representative is the Italian Perazzi (side-by-side or over-and-under), in which the mechanism can be dismounted merely by an extended movement of the safety catch. Ideal for cleaning and maintenance. Favours the attainment of good balance and handling quality.

OVER-AND-UNDER (USUALLY EJECTOR). Costly and beautiful versions of these guns are made by a few English makers—usually in sidelock form. Several cheaper Continental versions are available, including the famous F. N. Browning. The favourite of trap-shooters. Mechanism is less direct than in side-by-side, and loading is less easy. Weight is greater for equal duty.

SINGLE-BARRELLED, DROP-DOWN. Available in top quality for serious trap-shooting, but usually seen in cheap machine-made form. With cylinder boring and fitted with sights, becomes a valuable weapon for close-country deer shooting, using the rifled slug (see Chapter 14). Variable choke a useful addition (see Chapter 6). Mentionable here, as a variant is the Webley-Greener, Martini-action "G.P." gun—outstanding for strength and rearward disposition of weight, making for superior liveliness and balance. Preceding remarks on rifled slugs particularly apply.

PARADOX BALL AND SHOT GUN. This gun, usually a 12-bore side-by-side of normal appearance, except for its having sights, is in a category of its own. It is distinguished by having a short length of rifling at the muzzle end only of the barrels, and is capable of firing either a heavy (735 or 750 grain) bullet with the accuracy of an Express rifle, or a charge of small shot to a good cylinder pattern. The Paradox was particularly suitable for jungle shooting, and was effective against any soft-skinned dangerous game. It is now obsolete, as the special ammunition is no longer manufactured, but surviving specimens can make good use of the rifled slug (see page 120).

EJECTORS. When the double gun was being perfected in the 1890s, numerous ejectors were designed for throwing out the spent cartridge or cartridges. Notable examples are the Southgate, the Deeley and the Baker. The first has most deservedly and conspicuously survived. It comprises only two parts, as shown in fig. 4.

The mechanism is in duplicate—one set for each barrel—and is therefore fully selective: it operates only if the gun has been fired; and if one barrel only has been discharged then it ejects only the appropriate case.

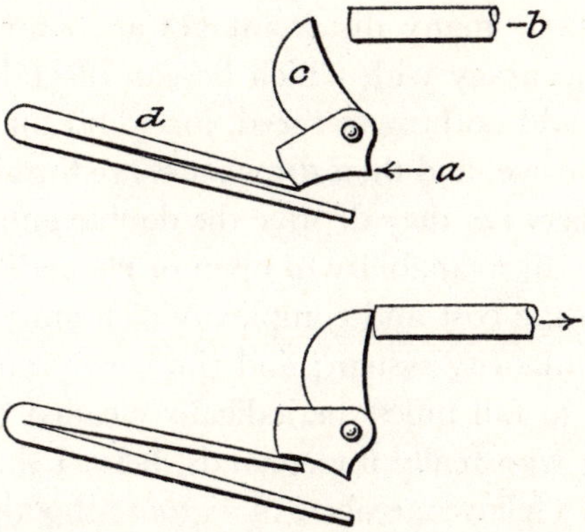

Fig. 4. The Southgate ejector, the simplest and by far the most popular of all ejectors, works on the over-centre principle, like the blade of a penknife. It comprises only two parts, the cam or "kicker" *c* and the vee-spring *d*. The top view shows it cocked and ready for action. When the gun is opened after firing, the end of the cocking lever, which projects from the knuckle of the action, engages the appropriate kicker at *a* and forces it around its pivot until the over-centre position is reached, whereupon the spring flicks it over (bottom) so that it strikes the end of the extractor rod *b* and ejects the appropriate cartridge. The re-closing of the gun forces the kicker back to the position shown in the top view.

As hitherto made, the ejector is always operative provided that the gun has been fired. But owing to the reloading potential of the now common plastic cartridges and to the indestructible litter they make if scattered on the ground, I have urged that ejectors should be made "optional", so that they can be switched out of action if the speed in reloading of which they admit is not called for by the sport in hand.

I am pleased to see that this suggestion is being taken up by some foreign gunmakers, and have myself published particulars* of a convenient way of converting the popular Spanish AYA guns from ordinary to optional ejection.

SINGLE TRIGGERS. These are optional on most high quality double guns. I regard them as a great mistake unless the shooter is satisfied that their many disadvantages are more than compensated by the accuracy with which he can place his second shot. They seem to add nothing to speed, for I find that the finger can usually beat the eye, and their drawbacks are formidable. Whether selective or otherwise, they deprive the double gun of its great advantage of instant availability of open or choke boring; they add appreciably to the cost and complexity of a gun; they habituate the user to a minority system; and they are prone to get out of adjustment or to fail unless periodically cleaned and overhauled by a gunsmith who really understands them. I shall never forget the lesson of two fellow-members of a grouse-shooting party in one of the remotest parts of the Highlands, whose single triggers failed them at the height of the season. The undoubted popularity of the single trigger in America, where it is widely regarded as a *sine qua non* on a good double gun, is due, I believe, to gadget-appeal, though it acquires merit as an aid to shooting in the colder regions, when fingers are numb.

RELEASE TRIGGERS. These triggers, practically unknown in this country, have a limited and possibly increasing following abroad. The trigger is pulled immediately *preparatory* to firing, and the shot is fired by letting the trigger go. Release triggers are claimed to be a cure for flinching (both physical and psychological forms) and are discussed further in Chapter 10 (Clay Pigeon Guns).

SELF-OPENING ACTIONS. Although personal preference is the deciding factor, no double gun is really up-to-date in my opinion unless it has a self-opening action. This not only adds to the pleasure of using the gun, but it materially increases personal

* "Case Salvage Made Easy", by Gough Thomas—*Shooting Times & Country Magazine*—June 21st, 1969

fire-power. I have repeatedly noticed in driven partridge shooting that with a self-opener I am able to reload more quickly than my next-in-line, if he is without that advantage. The most famous action of this sort is the Purdey, which is a true self-opener in the sense that irrespective of whether the gun has been fired or not, it opens by itself when the top lever is pushed over. Some guns, such as those with the classic Boss action, or the " Grand Clé " Darne,

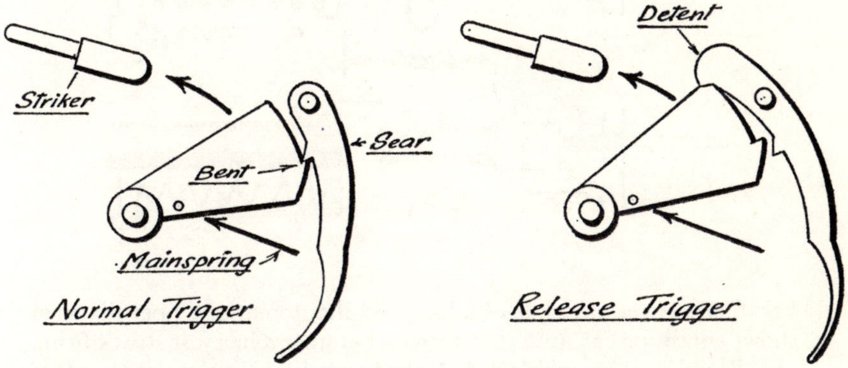

Fig. 5. Release trigger (diagrammatic only). Pulling the normal trigger (left) releases the hammer, which is then impelled by the mainspring to hit the striker and fire the gun. Pulling the release trigger (right) disengages sear from bent, but brings into action a detent which holds the hammer back until the trigger is released.

are self-openers when they have not been fired, easy-openers when one cartridge only has been fired, and neither when both have been fired. Others, such as the Westley Richards " Connaught " with the Smith action, are more accurately described as easy-openers. The distinction rests on whether, when both barrels have been discharged, the force of the mainspring (as in the Purdey) or of some auxiliary spring (as in the Holland & Holland and Lancaster " Twelve-Twenty " actions) is freely available for throwing open the gun, and whether it is adequate for that purpose.

REPEATERS

These are operated manually, by recoil or by gas pressure, and subdivide as follows.

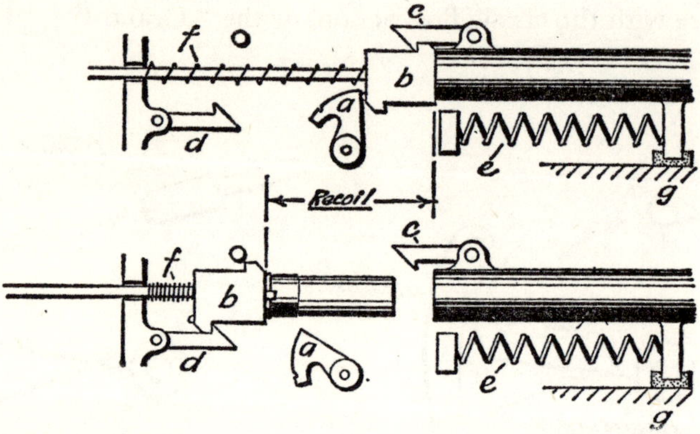

Fig. 6. Working principle of a long-recoil automatic. Upper diagram shows conditions at instant of firing—hammer *a* has just struck firing pin. Barrel and breechblock *b*, locked together, then recoil to extent indicated, recocking hammer in the process. (Part of energy of recoil is absorbed by friction brake *g*.) Breechblock lock *c* is then tripped and breechblock caught by latch *d*, as in lower diagram. Recoil spring *e* then returns barrel to original position, leaving empty case attached to breechblock by extractor hook, from which case is flicked sideways through ejection port by a projection on an extension (not shown) of the returning barrel. The returning barrel also trips the latch *d*, whereupon the action spring *f* restores breechblock to its original position, feeding a fresh cartridge into the chamber in the process. (Actual constructional details do not correspond to indications of the diagram.)
See also plate facing page 49.

(*a*) *Manually-operated repeaters.* The slide-action, trombone, or pump-gun, as it is variously called, and the bolt-action only need be considered under this head.

In the pump-gun the spent case is ejected and the gun recocked by pulling back the sliding fore-end. Pushing back the money he has available can best be spent on an English gun, a Continental one to a more elaborate specification, or an equivalent, but second-hand, one of English make.

Conventional gun or repeater?

I will deal with the first question first. It is one that causes heated controversy, which is a pity, because much of it arises out of ill-conceived attempts to dictate what is properly determinable by the tastes and fancies of others. I would offer it as an acceptable principle that *so far as a man shoots for pleasure, and shoots alone, the best gun for him is the one that serves his pleasure best, whether it be a repeater, a conventional gun or a muzzle-loader.* It is only so far as he shoots with others, or by their favour, that he owes any consideration to their views, and it may be, their prejudices. Prejudice undoubtedly exists. The young shooter or other newcomer to the sport must recognise that it is still strong against repeaters in regular shooting circles in this country. It arises from a feeling that such weapons are unethical or dangerous or both. What is worse, they are sometimes regarded as the mark of a greedy or unsporting shot. The fact that the prejudice may be without foundation is beside the point. What is much to the point is that a man who is in the way of receiving shooting invitations would miss many if he were known as a repeater man.

But the solitary wildfowler or rough shooter, or the clay pigeon enthusiast, need be deterred by none of these considerations—he can safely regulate his choice by the simple principle I have put forward. If he does not know, or cannot make up his mind, which kind of gun would best conform to that principle, I would recommend him to consider the various criteria by which a gun can be fairly judged and to make his decision accordingly.

The criteria in question are weight, recoil, balance and handling quality; ease of manipulation and safety; quietness of operation; ease of take-down and reassembly; ease of cleaning and general maintenance; portability and transportability. On a slightly different plane come reliability, durability and repairability. Different again are fire-power and adaptability; and yet again, beauty. I must comment on all these points.

Weight and recoil. These must be considered together. For a conventional gun or a manually-operated repeater, the minimum weight necessary to keep recoil within limits acceptable to the average man is usually taken as 96 times the weight of the shot charge—say 6 lb. for 1 oz. of shot, 6 lb. 6 oz. for $1\frac{1}{16}$ oz. and 6 lb. 12 oz. for $1\frac{1}{8}$ oz. Anything in excess of this is unnecessary in a game gun because conventional guns can readily be built down to these figures. But most other types cannot, or are not available in such weights. They should be marked down accordingly. Extra weight may not tell in a gunmaker's shop, but it will at the end of a long day, however young you may be. It is a characteristic of young men to tend to over-gun themselves; but they invariably learn to regard it as a great mistake, as I myself did. Indeed, if a shooter has to walk long distances for a few shots he may do well to submit to rather more recoil in order to enjoy the advantages of a lighter gun.

In the case of automatics, the 96 : 1 relationship may be affected by other considerations, which are dealt with in Chapter 9.

Balance and handling quality. This most desirable attribute of a gun is hard to over-rate. A well-balanced gun seems to join eagerly in the game, whereas a badly-balanced one hangs inertly on the hands in a spirit of complete non-co-operation. The subject of balance is so important that I have devoted the whole of Chapter 12 to it. Here I will merely say that the better conventional doubles, the Darne, the Greener G.P., the bolt-action repeater and the F. N. Browning 2-shot *with the aluminium alloy barrel* are the best-balanced and fastest-handling guns I have tested, though there are tactile aspects of balance, referred to in the chapter on the subject, from which some of these guns appear in a less favourable light.

Ease of manipulation and safety. These two also are bound up together. A gun should be easy to open and close. It should be equally easy to load *and unload*; and it should be particularly easy to check that it is indeed unloaded. From both the safety and convenience aspects, easy unloading is essential. When

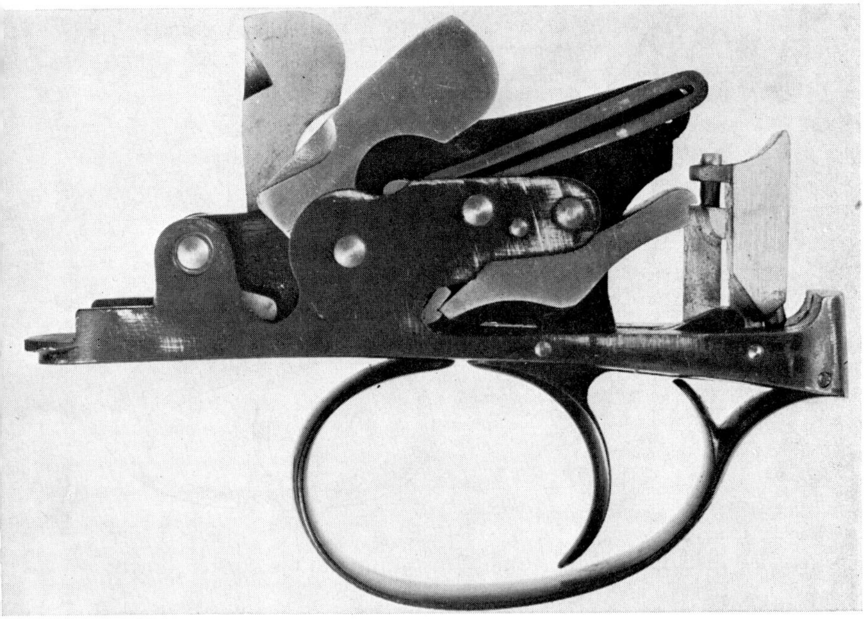

The trigger plate percussion mechanism of a Perazzi gun

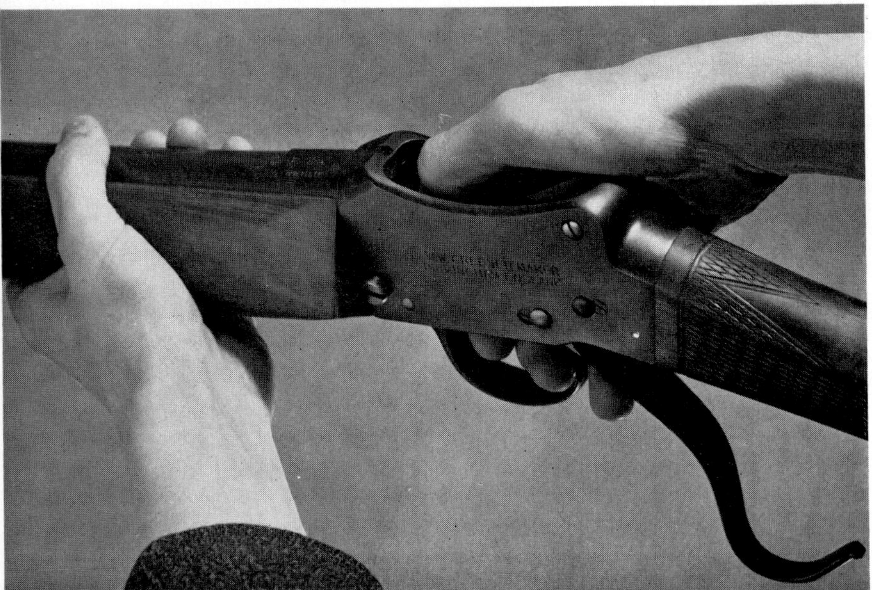

The Webley-Greener Martini action G.P. gun, a notably strong, durable and well-balanced weapon of its grade

A typical London-pattern sidelock gun incorporating locks as shown in fig. 3 and (usually) a Southgate ejector as shown in fig. 4

The Holland & Holland self-opening mechanism. A spring-loaded plunger with a forked end (top) fits in the fore-end of the gun (bottom) and presses against the upper edge of the knuckle of the action, as indicated by the arrows, thus throwing the gun open whenever the locking bolt is withdrawn

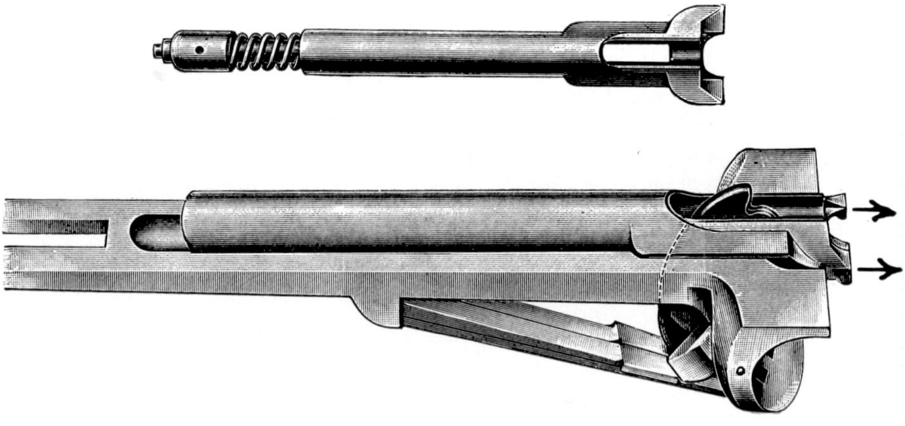

shooting over cultivated land, with its gates and ditches, it is necessary to unload very frequently—how frequently I never realised until the day when an unconventional weapon caused me considerable inconvenience in this respect. Unfortunately, it is not enough to make your gun safe by merely operating the safety device provided by the manufacturers. Your friends know nothing of the efficacy of such devices: *they want ocular evidence that your gun has been emptied,* or that it has been made demonstrably safe, as by the dropping of the barrels of a conventional gun. If the kind of gun you are using does not enable you to afford them that satisfaction, you may find yourself being avoided. Prejudice apart, this is one of the good reasons for the unpopularity of repeaters in the shooting field. For what they are worth, safety catches should be accessible without changing the grip on the weapon, and their state should be instantly visible and capable of being checked by touch alone. (See also Chapter 14.)

Finally, it should be easy to check, even in bad light, that the barrels are free from obstruction—particularly mud and snow. All the repeaters and the Darne are at a disadvantage here.

Quietness of operation. To avoid putting game on the *qui vive*, it is always desirable and frequently necessary to load or unload silently. This is easy with a conventional gun, but most repeaters are noisy in all their operations.

Ease of take-down and reassembly. This is important from the safety as well as from the convenience point of view. If a gun does not come to pieces with the ease of the conventional type, there is a temptation to keep it together—in a motor car, for example; and one day, there may be a cartridge left in it.

Ease of cleaning and general maintenance. The barrels of a gun should be instantly and conveniently demountable, or otherwise made accessible, for cleaning and inspection. Ideally, this should also apply to the breech-locking, percussion and ejector systems, which should be separable from the woodwork for drying out by warmth, or for immersion in cleaning or lubricating baths. The Darne and the bolt-action repeater alone fully conform to this ideal, but are closely followed by the sidelock.

The box-lock and the remaining repeaters are less easy of access to their internal parts.

It must always be remembered that guns get very wet at times and that, if many cartridges are fired, impacted water is likely to become sprayed into every part of the weapon. Small coil springs can quickly rust through if water is allowed to remain in their working cavities; and there are no less than fifteen coil springs, large and small, tucked away in one of the most popular of the automatics.

Portability. A gun is not always in the hands. It has to be carried for long walks in the crook of the arm or triggers-upwards over the shoulder. A gun which cannot be carried thus in comfort is not a good shooting companion. Bottom-ejection repeaters, in which the underpart of the receiver is reduced to two narrow rails, need critical regard from this point of view. When its breech is closed (but not otherwise), the Darne, with its rearward weight and broad wooden bar, is the most comfortable of all guns to carry, with the ordinary doubles running it very close.

Transportability. A gun should pack away in a small case for easy transport by motor car.

Reliability, durability and repairability. The reliability and durability of the conventional gun are a byword. Cases within my knowledge that come immediately to mind are a B.S.A. that went straight back into service after being recovered from the muddy bottom of an African river; an old Gallyon pinfire which was *ploughed up* on the glebe of a sporting parson friend of mine, and which he used for some years after merely having it cleaned and re-proved; and a Boss sidelock which has survived the firing of some $1\frac{1}{2}$ million rounds in the testing department of the Kynoch works without appreciable deterioration. There may be comparable cases of repeaters, but I have never heard of them. The pump gun is known to be a durable weapon, but not so the self-loaders, which have a comparatively short trouble-free life. The latter are also prone to malfunctioning from a number of causes, including swollen or malformed cartridges and sand or mud in the mechanism, to which the open, cage-like receivers of some types are particularly accessible.

It should not be overlooked that a broken spring or the like, which may put one barrel of a double gun out of action, is unlikely to affect the other, so that the weapon is not wholly incapacitated by such an accident.

The ease and speed with which a weapon can be repaired is an important consideration. The great bulk of the repairs required to conventional guns are broken springs and dented barrels, with which any practical gunsmith in this country can cope. Whether he would be so competent to deal with the repair and adjustment of repeaters is open to some doubt, and the prospective purchaser of one of these guns would do well to check this point with his local gunsmith.

Any unusual materials or modes of construction in a gun should be critically regarded from the repairability point of view. For example, the removal of dents from chromed barrels presents difficulties (see Chapter 14); and dents in fibre glass or aluminium alloy barrels would fox many a practical repairer.

Fire-power and adaptability. I believe it is generally admitted by those who have taken the trouble to make the experiment that the *sustained* fire-power of a conventional hammerless ejector is greater than that of a 5-shot self-loader—in other words, that over a period one can get off more shots with the former than with the latter. It is argued for the repeater that where birds are coming in bunches at short intervals the user of a 5-shot repeater is nevertheless at an advantage; but it is not explained how the bunches are persuaded to time their arrival so as to avoid the occasions when he has only one or two cartridges in his magazine, or the relatively long periods required to replenish it.

The adaptability of the repeater, with its single barrel, can be extended by the fitting of a variable choke. Not so the double. But then the latter, if a two-triggered weapon, offers an *instant* choice of choke or open boring, as well as a similar choice of shot sizes, or even shot and ball. This last can be a valuable feature abroad, where dangerous big game may turn up unexpectedly in a drive.

Beauty. I make no apology for adding beauty to my list of desiderata. A gun is, so to speak, an intimately manual implement which has to be used with speed and precision. It should thus possess in the highest possible degree the quality of conforming instantly to its user's intentions, without distracting him in any way from the object of his pursuit. This requires that it should not only be light and well-balanced, and smooth and elegant, but that its form and proportions should be altogether in harmony with the muscular reactions and tactile sense of the shooter. If it possesses all these qualities, the gun will have functional beauty—a kind of beauty that may be observed in many things that have become perfectly adapted over the centuries to human use and handling. What we are concerned with here is no mere whimsy, but the last refinement of efficiency. It is a kind of beauty that may be seen to perfection in a fine English game gun, and is in no way dependent on applied adornment. Even cheap conventional guns, if well designed, can claim it in goodly measure. An example is the Spanish gun shown opposite page 15. But the broken lines of the repeaters shown, and in particular the gravid appearance of the automatics are, in my opinion, aesthetically painful and constitute a serious defect.

So much, therefore, for the factors to be considered by the uncommitted shooter in choosing a gun for general rough shooting in this country. If I were asked for a recommendation, I could only say that, on the counts I have listed, the side-by-side double seems to me to be by far the superior weapon.

A harsh evolution

This is hardly surprising, for few mechanical inventions can ever have been subjected to such a harsh process of evolution. It was, as I have already indicated, developed empirically over many decades by a highly inventive and highly competitive trade to meet the needs of a world market, including, at one extreme, a large social class of wealthy and critical customers, who, regardless of cost, demanded the highest degree of functional efficiency combined with outward elegance; and at the other, a multitude of humbler gunners, ranging from the rabbiting rustic of the home country to the hunters, traders and prospectors of the new dependencies beyond the seas. Both these classes subjected their guns to gruelling conditions of service: the first by the large number of cartridges they fired—five to ten thousand in a season was not uncommon—and the second by exposing them to every hazard that rough treatment and neglect could possibly entail. Yet the double gun not only survived these extremes of usage, but proved itself to have a liberal margin of endurance and dependability, so that even when worn, neglected, out of proof, and shaking in all its joints, it could still continue to withstand the shocks and stresses of discharge.

So far as the type of weapon is concerned, therefore, the game or skeet shooter, the wildfowler or pigeon shot, who chooses a conventional gun can hardly go wrong. The serious trap-shooter will probably choose the over-and-under version, but the others are likely to be better suited with the side-by-side. In its most highly developed form, which, in my opinion, is the London pattern sidelock with rebounding locks and self-opening action, it will cost as much as a motor car, though it will last a lifetime and cost next to nothing to maintain. For £250, it is nevertheless possible to buy a superior English box-lock gun; and £150 will buy one that is still thoroughly sound and well made in every respect. For £75 or so one can buy an honest and seemly foreign gun such as that last referred to. But these are January 1970 figures, and gun prices appear to be doubling about every ten years.

As for the more general question of English versus foreign guns, it is widely recognised that some wage rates abroad are so far below ours as to give the makers an important economic advantage. This, however, is partly offset by import duty, and by the existence of makers of bad, cheap guns who are out to exploit the demand that has been created in this country by their more reputable compatriots. The buyer's protection is to confine his choice to guns offered and recommended by an established retailer, preferably a member of the Gun Trade Association, who thereby covers them by his own implied warranty as to fitness for purpose. Such warranty, I am advised, is fully valid in law.

Second-hand guns present a more difficult problem. Good second-hand guns are becoming increasingly scarce and dear. " Gun coping " is much on the increase, and the path of the inexpert buyer is beset by pitfalls. For example, guns can be tightened by unsound or even dishonest methods whereby they shoot loose again after a few shots. They may be lapped to remove pitting until they are out of proof; or lapped to the verge of proof without quite successfully removing all of the pitting. An unscrupulous vendor might then assert that the pitting is a trifling blemish which could easily be removed at any time. So it might seem until the barrel is gauged, when it would be apparent that any further lapping would involve re-proof, with all its attendant risks and expense. Unless, therefore, a prospective purchaser is particularly astute and well informed, he should avoid transactions with unknown private individuals, or at least insist on having any gun offered by such a one scrupulously vetted by a first-class practical gunsmith. He should refuse even to look at a " bargain " offered at a low price for a quick sale by a stranger who is reluctant to afford him the opportunity of thus having the gun checked; and for the rest, he should confine his choice to guaranteed weapons offered by such a retailer as I have described.

For my own part, I would rather buy a second-hand gun straight off the field, with all its blemishes and signs of wear, than after it had been done-up by someone I did not know and trust implicitly.

CHAPTER FOUR

CHOICE OF A GUN (PERFORMANCE)

We now come to those questions of power and range which logically come first in the choice of a gun, but which I deferred in the last chapter for the reasons indicated. Although most men requiring a gun for general rough shooting in this country can safely short-circuit these questions and go straight for an ordinary 12-bore, there are others who cannot do so—not, that is to say, if they want to get the best satisfaction from their sport. They are chiefly those who pursue their game under exceptionally difficult conditions, arising out of the kind of territory they shoot over, or the nature and habits of the game concerned, or even out of some physical limitation or disability of their own. They may well require something different from the standard 12-bore game gun firing a standard charge, such as would best suit the general rough shooter. There is also to be considered the man who inherits or acquires a non-standard gun, and needs some knowledge of its potentialities.

So we come down to the fundamental requirements of a gun for a particular class of sport, which are above and beyond any question of the type of mechanism it possesses for opening and closing the breech, etc. These requirements can only be determined by the kind of game mainly in view and the maximum range at which it must normally be taken for its effective pursuit. This poses straightaway the question of how to specify the range of a gun. That is easy, one might say: the range of a gun is simply its maximum killing range.

But that would never do, because birds may occasionally be killed by individual pellets finding a vital spot at distances far in excess of the gun's normal reach. Regularly used at such distances, it would produce a dismal record of misses, relieved—if that is the right word—by a few instances of birds being hit, but not killed, and going off merely pricked, or maybe wounded, with one or two pellets in non-vital parts. In the process, the shooter would endure endless frustration, and would experience, we may hope, many qualms of conscience.

Clearly then, both on ethical and practical grounds it is necessary to abandon any conception of the maximum killing range of a gun, and to substitute that of the maximum effective range, which, unlike the former, can at least be defined. Thus, *the maximum effective range of a gun in relation to a given kind of game is the greatest range at which it is reasonably certain that a clean kill will be made by a truly aimed shot,* it being understood that the size of shot used will be within the range of sizes normally employed for that particular purpose.

Even so, it will be noted that the definition lacks precision, because of that word " reasonably ". But it cannot be omitted, for even with the most accurate shooting, and guns and cartridges giving unexceptionable performance, there will inevitably be marked variations in the number and location of the pellets striking a target of given size at a given distance. The maximum effective range of a gun and load against a particular kind of game is not, in fact, a specific distance—it depends partly on what sort of performance the shooter is prepared to accept. If he demands 100 kills from 100 accurately aimed shots, he must be prepared to regard his gun as having a shorter effective range than that commonly assumed. I shall return to this point a little later.

But having defined it, how is the maximum effective range to be determined? As an experimental addict, I have always found the question a baffling one, inasmuch as it cannot be answered out of hand by direct practical trial. If one took a particular gun into a country thick with the appropriate kind of game, and shot it hard for a whole season, it would not be possible to extract the required answer from the record. In the first place, since the effective range merges insensibly into the region of flukes, it would be impossible to say whether distant birds struck dead *ought* to have been struck dead or whether they were merely unlucky. Conversely, it could not be said whether those that escaped did so because of the inadequacy of the weapon or the unskilfulness of the shooter. And then there would remain the overall practical difficulty of saying in each case what exactly was the range from the gun to bird in mid-air. (How do some shooters decide, I wonder, that such and such a bird was killed, say, "fully 70 yards off?" If it means, as it usually does, that it was 70 *paces* from the shooter's position to the point at which the bird fell, the account is not of much value to the serious enquirer.)

The Burrard method

In the circumstances, it seems that the method followed by Burrard, in his well-known and painstaking attempt to find a general answer to the question of the effective range of shotguns, is the most feasible one. What Burrard did was to measure the sizes of various birds, or, more strictly, the areas covered by their vulnerable regions, and to regard these as targets which he then proceeded to relate to the known pattern distribution of various guns. Then, having decided from experience how many pellets could be taken as a minimum to ensure a clean kill, he was able to calculate the minimum patterns necessary to achieve this purpose. The greatest distance at which a given gun with a given load would be capable of throwing such a pattern could thus be taken as its maximum effective range. There is no theory involved in the method—it merely puts together two sets of practical measurements. The results had, of necessity, to be hedged in within limits prescribed by the minimum striking energy of the individual pellets. Also a 10 per cent allowance had to be made for stringing. The calculations, as finally worked out by I.M.I. for a standard 2½-inch 12-bore, are summarised in a well-known table published in *The Shooter's Year Book*. They assume that the minimum requirements for a clean kill are:

Small Birds, such as snipe—2 pellets, each having a striking energy of at least 0.5 ft. lb.

Medium Birds, such as grouse—3 pellets, each having a striking energy of at least 0.85 ft. lb.

Large Birds, such as geese—4 pellets, each having a striking energy of at least 1.5 ft. lb.

This table has stood unchanged for many years, and undoubtedly gives a widely accepted picture of the capacity of a standard 12-bore. Such reservations as I have come to acquire since the first edition of this book can be dealt with conveniently later.

In the meantime, to fulfil the original purpose of this chapter, we must go further. We are trying to arrive at some general guidance in the choice of a gun for a particular class of sport, and it may be found in a more general application of the Burrard principle. Proceeding by his method, it is easy to work out certain minimum patterns as being necessary to ensure that sufficient pellets are likely to strike the kind of bird concerned

TABLE 1. Minimum Patterns (including allowance for stringing)

Game	*Shot Size*	*Minimum Pattern in a 30-inch circle*
Snipe	8	270
Woodcock	7	150
Squirrel	7	180
Partridge	6	130
Grouse	6	130
Pheasant	6	120
Pigeon	6	130
Rabbit	5	120
Teal	5	110
Duck	4	80
Hare	4	100
Goose	3	70

(*Note*: The above minimum patterns are subject to the preceding remarks on minimum pellet energy—see also Table 3.)

to bring about a clean kill. They come out as in Table 1, which, for consistency's sake, I have back-calculated from *The Shooter's Year Book* table and rounded off.

If, to this information, we now add particulars of the percentage patterns at all ranges thrown by guns of different boring, we shall find ourselves in a position to give at least a *prima facie* answer to a considerable variety of questions on shotgun range and performance. The required further particulars are those set out in the following table, which I have reproduced from *The Shooter's Year Book*.

TABLE 2. Percentage Patterns for all Borings at all Ranges

Boring of Gun	*Range in yards* 30	35	40	45	50	55	60
True Cyl.	60	49	40	33	27	22	18
Imp. Cyl.	72	60	50	41	33	27	22
¼ Choke	77	65	55	46	38	30	25
½ Choke	83	71	60	50	41	33	27
¾ Choke	91	77	65	55	46	37	30
Full Choke	100	84	70	59	49	40	32

In order that individual pellet energies may be checked where necessary against the minimum figures already quoted, I give them for all ranges and sizes in Table 3 below.

TABLE 3. Striking Energy in foot-pounds for Individual Pellets fired at Observed Velocity of 1,070 feet per second

Size of Shot	*Range in yards* 30	35	40	45	50	55	60
3	4.48	3.92	3.43	2.99	2.59	2.23	1.94
4	3.54	3.08	2.66	2.30	1.97	1.68	1.42
5	2.60	2.23	1.90	1.61	1.36	1.14	0.93
6	2.03	1.71	1.44	1.20	1.01	0.82	0.67
7	1.52	1.27	1.06	0.86	0.70	0.57	0.45

(*N.B. The energies listed are true only of those pellets that have preserved their original form and substance intact.*)

We can now say what charge of shot is needed to deal effectively with a given kind of game at a given range; and with that information to say what kind of gun is required to throw it.

Example 1. A shooter wants a gun for flighting duck which he must be prepared to take at 55 yards. From Table 1 we see that a mallard needs a minimum pattern of 80 pellets in the standard 30-inch circle. Let us assume No. 4 shot and full-choke boring; we then see from Table 2 that at 55 yards a full-choke gives only a 40 per cent pattern. So the 80 pellets we require will be 40 per cent of the total charge. The total charge will accordingly be $\frac{80 \times 100}{40}$ or 200 pellets. Now 200 pellets of No. 4 is almost exactly $1\frac{3}{16}$ oz., which contains 202 pellets (see Table 4), and our shooter will thus need a gun capable of handling $1\frac{3}{16}$ oz. of No. 4 shot. This is just the capacity of a $2\frac{1}{2}$-inch 12-bore with a Maximum cartridge; but as there would be absolutely no reserve with this combination, the appropriate choice would be a gun capable of firing $1\frac{1}{4}$ oz., namely, a $2\frac{3}{4}$-inch 12-bore, which is therefore the gun required. It should weigh not less than 96 times $1\frac{1}{4}$ oz. (see Chapter 9) or $7\frac{1}{2}$ lb. unless, owing to the few shots that may be fired, the shooter is prepared to accept more recoil.

Example 2. As an opposite case, consider a man who requires a gun for driven partridges for which he prefers No. 6 shot and is fully content with a maximum effective range of 40 yards. If we assume improved cylinder boring as being desirable to make the most of the shooter's chances, we get the following result.

Minimum pattern required (Table 1) = 130
Improved cyl. pattern at 40 yards (Table 2) = 50 per cent

$$\text{Therefore total charge} = \frac{130 \times 100}{50} = 260 \text{ pellets}$$

Two hundred and sixty pellets of No. 6 weigh just short of 1 oz. (270 pellets), which is an ideal charge for a light 12-bore, weighing, with 27- or 28-inch barrels, 6 lb. 2 oz. to 6 lb. 4 oz. As the shooter will probably fire a considerable number of cartridges in warm weather when the ballistics of some cartridges are at a maximum, the indications are in favour of a gun of about the latter weight.

Practical shooters may here object that it does not need

calculations to show a duck flighter that he ought to use a long-cased, fully-choked 12-bore, or a partridge shooter that the right gun for him is a lightly-loaded, open-bored gun of the same calibre. I would entirely agree; and I have used these particular examples precisely because the answers can be so readily checked from common knowledge and to give confidence in the method as yielding useful guidance where common knowledge might fail.

The young or elderly shooter, the partially disabled or the gun-headache sufferer, any one of whom might be prepared to make sacrifices to find a gun suited to his condition, might find the methods of this chapter an invaluable guide. So might the experimenter who likes to wander from the beaten track, or the man who is unable to shoot to his reasonable satisfaction with a fully-choked gun.

Further, the information can be used equally well to solve problems coming from the opposite angle—that is, when the gun is the known factor and the maximum effective performance is required.

Example 3 (*an actual case*). A shooter has inherited a beautiful pair of improved-cylinder bored Greener $2\frac{1}{2}$-inch 20-bores, which he wishes to use for partridges and grouse. What size of shot should he use, and what would be the effective range?

From Table 1, the minimum pattern required is 130

Normal charge for a $2\frac{1}{2}$-inch 20-bore ... ... $\frac{13}{16}$ oz.

(a) Try, first, No. 6 shot

Total pellets in charge 219

Required pattern is $\frac{130}{219} \times 100$ per cent of this, or ... ... 60 per cent.

From Table 2, a 60 per cent pattern is seen to be just about the capacity of an improved cylinder at 35 yards; and at this distance the pellet energy is seen from Table 3 to be 1.71 ft. lb. as against the minimum of 0.85 stated to be required for medium birds.

So with No. 6 shot, pattern is only just adequate at 35 yards, but pellet energy is still well up. The indications are in favour of a smaller size of shot.

(b) Try, then, No. 7 shot

Total pellets in charge 276

Required pattern is $\frac{130}{276} \times 100$ per cent

of this, or ... ... 47 per cent.

From Table 2, a 47 per cent pattern is seen to be within the capacity of an improved cylinder at 40 yards. Pellet energy of No. 7 at this range is 1.06 ft. lb.—just above the 0.85 minimum.

Clearly, any smaller size of shot would fail on pellet energy; so the answer required is No. 7 shot and 40 yards. But there is obviously so little reserve at this range that it would have to be regarded as the absolute maximum. My advice to the enquirer was therefore No. 7 shot and 35-40 yards.

Comprehensive performance diagram

So much for the Burrard method as applied. The acceptability of the results depends, as explained, on what the shooter may regard as reasonably consistent performance. On the latest evidence in my possession, I would prefer to reduce somewhat the ranges given in the I.M.I. table and in the preceding examples, and have done so in what follows.

Also, although the minimum pellet energies specified are believed to be adequate for medium game birds, up to the size, say, of grouse, they should be stepped up for larger birds, such as cock pheasants, which I consider need 1.5 foot-pounds for reasonable results. Duck (e.g. mallard) also need 1.5. The smaller geese should be allowed 2, whilst to do the right thing by the big Canadas needs fully 3.

With a view to providing some broader guidance to shotgun performance than that afforded by the examples previously given, I append a diagram showing the maximum effective range attainable by various charges of shot, irrespective of the calibre of the guns from which they are fired, provided only that they are fired to a good, regular pattern and at not materially less

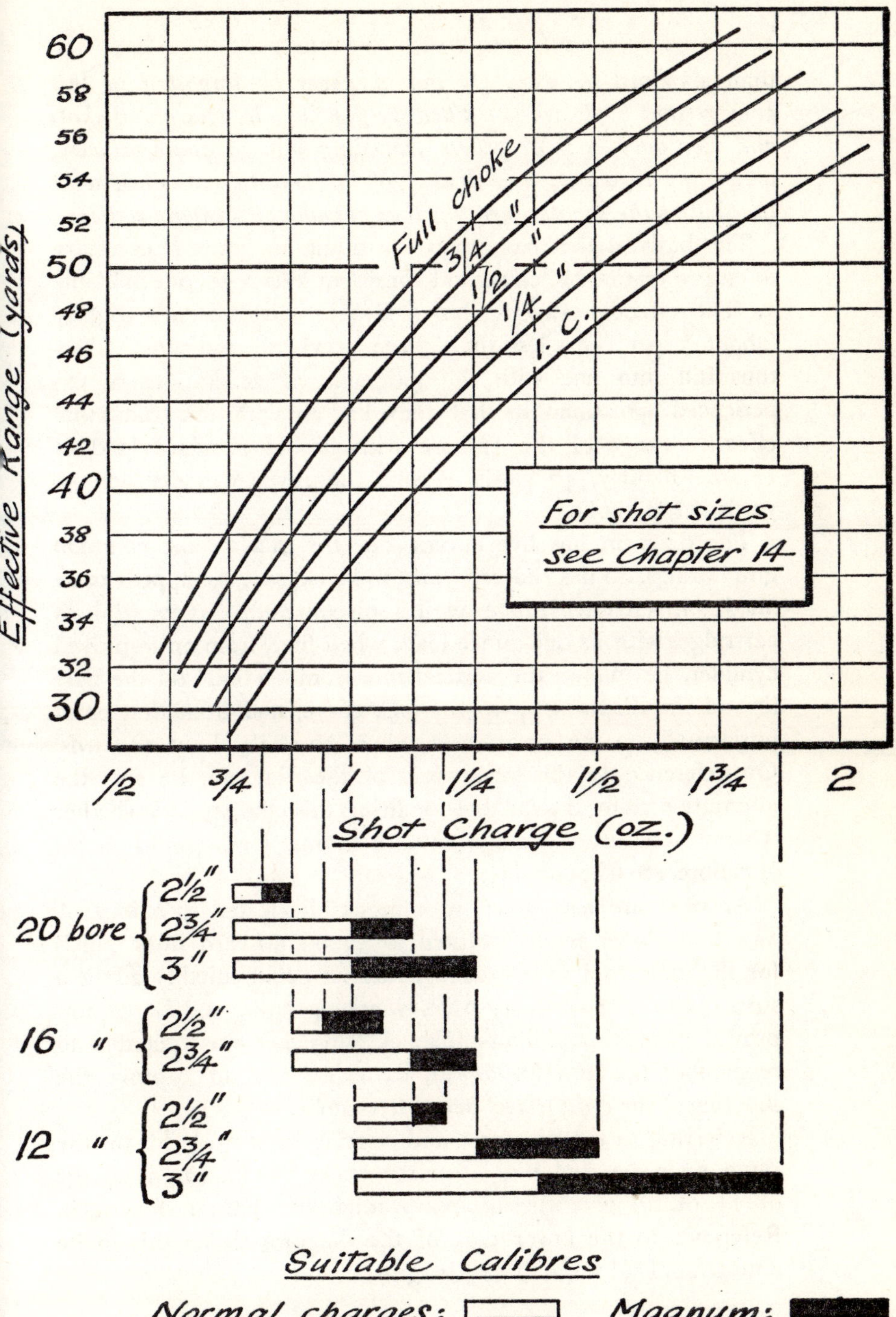

Fig. 8. Effective ranges of various guns and loads

than standard velocity. (*It should never be forgotten in this context that birds are not killed by guns but by charges of shot, and then only by those pellets, travelling with adequate velocity, which the regularity and density of the pattern, combined with the skill of the shooter, are together capable of bringing to bear.*)

The basis of the diagram is the minimum pattern necessary to ensure reasonably clean and consistent kills as set out in Table 1. The effective ranges shown by the diagram are slightly (about 7 per cent) less than those previously indicated. They thus full into line with the judgment of generations of experienced sportsmen in that they key in with the traditional effective range of the 12-bore with its old standard load of 1⅛ oz.—namely, 40 yards if bored improved cylinder and 50 yards if full choke.

The diagram has five curves, one for each of the common gun borings. So if a shooter wants to know, say, the approximate maximum effective range against pigeon of the 16ga. 2¾-inch cartridge, with its one-ounce load, when fired from an improved cylinder, he follows the vertical line from "1 oz." on the base line of the diagram up to the I.C. curve, and from that point horizontally to the range scale, where he reads about 38 yards. On reference to the lower part of the diagram, he sees the alternative calibres available for firing this charge, and whether it would constitute a magnum or a normal load. (As to choice of calibre, see Chapter 11.)

Answers are also given to more sophisticated questions. A *Shooting Times* reader wanted a "good 50-yard duck gun" for flighting, and wondered whether he could suitably adapt a strong, heavy 2½-inch 12-bore, weighing 7 lb. and bored improved cylinder and half-choke. A gunmaker was prepared to rechamber the gun for 2¾ in. cartridges and to improve the shooting of the right barrel to quarter-choke.

Referring to the diagram, and starting from 50 yards on the range scale, we find that a quarter-choke would need a charge of 1½ oz. to give the necessary minimum pattern for duck. Reference to the lower part of the diagram shows this to be a magnum load for a 12 × 2¾ in. gun.

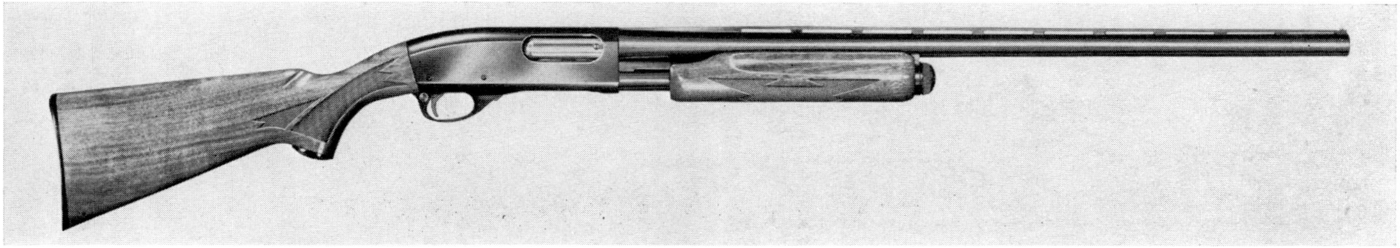

A typical American pump gun. The model shown is the popular Remington M. 870

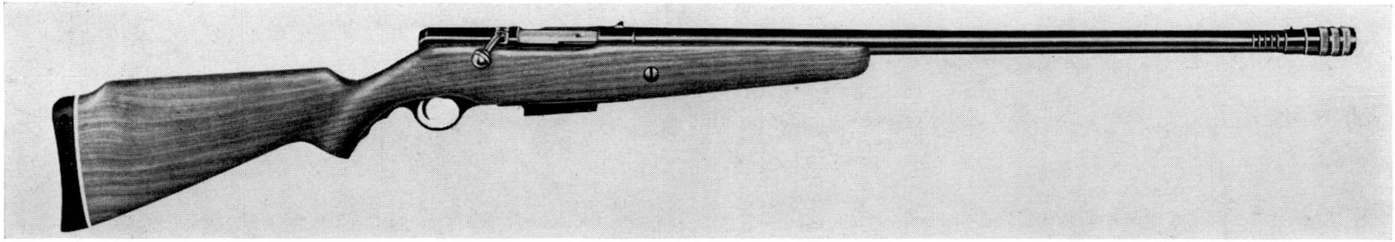

An American bolt action repeater. This Mossberg gun is fitted with a collet-type variable choke. Guns of this kind are usually among the most inexpensive of shotguns, but possess the merits inseparable from the basic design

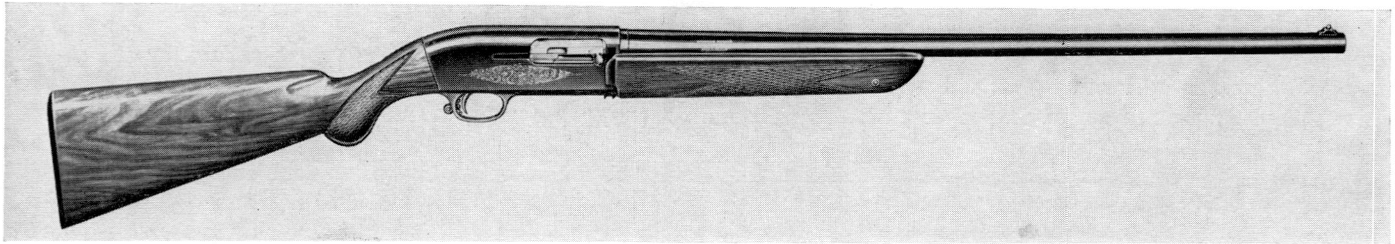

The F.N. Browning short-recoil (2-shot) automatic, introduced in direct competition with the conventional double-barrelled gun—see also fig. 7

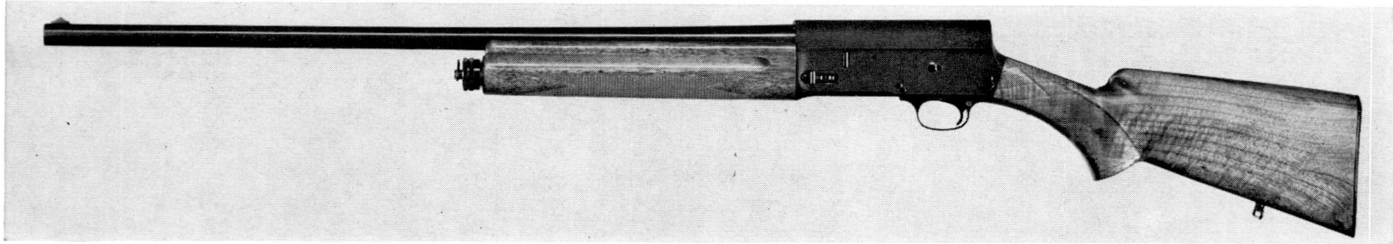

The F.N. Browning long-recoil automatic. The first self-loading shotgun working on the long-recoil principle, and still one of the favourites. See also fig. 6

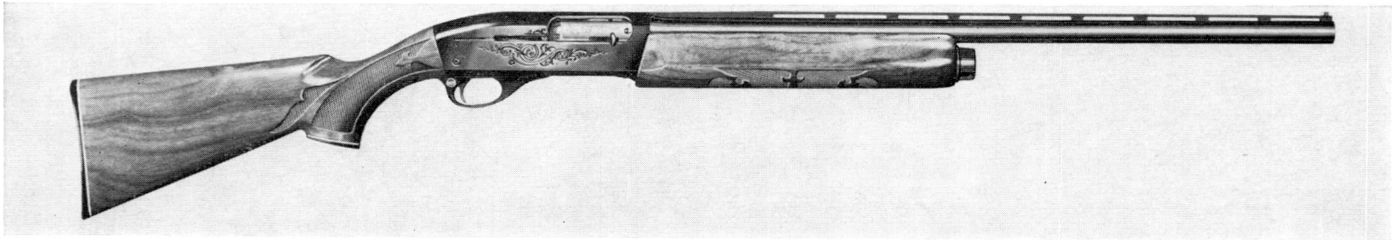

A typical American gas-operated automatic shotgun, the Remington 1100. The gas cylinder which

The practical limit, having regard to the $3\frac{1}{4}$ tons maximum working pressure for which the gun would normally be re-proved, and the heavy recoil of magnum charges in a gun of this weight (see Chapter 9), would be the $1\frac{1}{4}$ oz. Alphamax, which can be seen from the diagram to have an effective range of about 45 yards with a quarter-choke and 47 yards with a half-choke.

In working out this diagram, I have assumed that the shot sizes are those popularly used, as stated.

Owing to the rapid deterioration of patterns at extended distances, I have not attempted to legislate for ranges in excess of 60 yards.

TABLE 4. Pellets in Game Charges

Oz. of Shot	*Size of Shot* 3	4	5	6	7	8
$1\frac{1}{2}$	210	255	330	405	510	675
$1\frac{7}{16}$	201	244	316	388	489	646
$1\frac{3}{8}$	192	234	303	371	468	618
$1\frac{5}{16}$	183	223	289	354	446	590
$1\frac{1}{4}$	175	213	275	338	425	562
$1\frac{3}{16}$	166	202	261	321	404	534
$1\frac{1}{8}$	157	191	248	304	383	506
$1\frac{1}{16}$	149	181	234	287	361	478
1	140	170	220	270	340	450
$\frac{15}{16}$	131	159	206	253	319	422
$\frac{7}{8}$	122	149	193	236	298	394
$\frac{13}{16}$	113	138	179	219	276	366
$\frac{3}{4}$	105	128	165	202	255	338
$\frac{11}{16}$	96	117	151	186	234	310
$\frac{5}{8}$	87	106	138	169	212	282
$\frac{9}{16}$	78	96	124	152	191	254
$\frac{1}{2}$	70	85	110	135	170	225

I am well aware that some shooters, and particularly wild-fowlers, will regard the ranges given by these diagrams as being inferior to those of their favourite guns and cartridges; and it must be admitted that the large sizes of shot used against duck and geese retain sufficient energy to score kills well outside the effective range if only a lucky pellet hits a vital spot. But deliberate reliance on this kind of happening is not sport and cannot be taken into account in any serious study of the effective power and range of a sporting gun. Wildfowlers should pattern their guns at the range at which they believe them to be effective. They will not fail to note the rapid deterioration in pattern density and quality; and if they are using the maximum charges their guns are capable of shooting, they may well find that the dense part of their full choke patterns is passing well below the point of aim.

Particulars of the number of pellets in game charges, as needed for performance calculations, are given in Table 4.

A necessary warning

The preceding diagram and examples must not be taken for more than they are worth. The maximum effective range of a shotgun being partly dependent on the shooter's interpretation of that word "reasonably" (page 40), the diagram is best regarded as affording a broad picture of the range and power of various guns and loads and especially their *comparative* effectiveness. It shows more accurately, and perhaps more revealingly than anything else, the relatively small gains due to increased or magnum loads. *It will be seen that every extra eighth of an ounce of shot is worth only 3 or 4 yards in terms of range*—a distance too small to be judged in the air, and under the varying conditions of light and background met with in the course of shooting.

There is a further point. Calculations like those on which this diagram and the preceding examples are based depend absolutely for their realism on guns and cartridges that not only give approximately standard performances in terms of velocity and percentage patterns at stated ranges, *but which also give patterns of good uniform quality.* If the patterns are appreciably below standard in quality or pellet-count, as they may be with cartridges that are bad or unsuited to the gun, or with a gun that is badly bored or otherwise defective, then the calculations are without practical significance. Patterns frequently fail before velocity, and invariably so with the larger sizes of shot, and no sportsman can afford to be indifferent to the patterns thrown by his gun and cartridges unless he is content to take his game at short range or to depend on fluke shots. I deal with these points more fully later.

But subject to these remarks, the foregoing conclusions would, I think, be endorsed by any experienced shooter; and, so far as they go, they confirm the practical nature of the method employed and its applicability to a wide range of problems involved in the choice of a gun.

CHAPTER FIVE

PATTERNS

In the last chapter I think I made it clear that for consistent and predictable performance, it is necessary to have patterns reasonably conforming to the nominal boring of the gun and also of good, uniform quality. If the actual performance falls conspicuously below this ideal, the shooter is left to a greater or less extent in the dark. Let us consider the practical effect of bad, patchy patterns on the performance of a competent shot, who is taking all his birds within what he has a right to regard as a fair sporting range for the gun and cartridges in question. Some birds will be caught with a dense part of the pattern. These will be struck decisively dead even if well out towards the limiting range, and will impress the shooter as indicating that his gun is good and his cartridges thoroughly effective. But other birds, at all ranges, struck by weak, open parts of the pattern, will either escape or go off pricked or feathered or with a leg down. The baffled shooter will not know who or what to blame, though it is all too likely in the circumstances that he will blame himself, and thereby start a hoodoo which may take weeks to get rid of.

Good patterns are supremely important for long range work. The wildfowler shooting flighting duck or geese at maximum range is particularly dependent on pattern quality. Express and magnum loads and high velocity have a deadlier sound than pattern, but it is the pattern that tells. *This, as I have already indicated, is because the wildfowler's patterns fail before velocity* —a fact which should never be lost sight of by the long-range shooter.

A practical test

Some years ago I examined in the *Shooting Times* the claim of an American author respecting some of his compatriots who were stated to be "constantly dropping mallard well out towards the 80-yard mark with their trusty 12-gauges". For this purpose I arranged for a test to be carried out, in the course of which five shots were fired from a new, fully-choked, $2\frac{3}{4}$-inch 12-bore, bearing the name of a world-famous American maker, from a carefully measured distance of 80 yards. The cartridges were a premium grade, loaded with $1\frac{1}{2}$oz. of American No. 4 shot, corresponding to English No. 3. I reproduce in fig. 13 the best of the five diagrams. It will be seen that the pattern at this range had utterly failed, and that it must have failed a good way back. More than half the pellets never reached the six-foot target, and those that did had no recognisable pattern-centre. Nevertheless, the individual pellets, though much depleted of their original velocity and energy, had still retained about 1.0 ft. lb., which is the same as the minimum still sometimes accepted. This is, therefore, an extreme case in point; for at the stage when velocity might still have been just adequate, pattern had gone, and with it, any assurance of an effective shot.

Does it matter?

Before considering the factors that affect pattern, it might be well to consider the views of the practical sceptics who deprecate all discussion of patterns as being totally unnecessary, morbidly introspective and bad for shooting. Some may declare that any kind of cartridge does for them, provided it makes a bang, and they may appear to justify themselves by performing admirably in the field. But I have never known these men to seek out bad cartridges. If they take the first that come, they probably get good ones nearly every time. I know that if I went into my village shop and asked for some 12-gauge cartridges—"anything you've got will do"—I should get *Grand Prix* No. 6s. And even if they were something inferior, I might do better with them than another man with the best, if only I were a good enough shot to take my birds consistently with the centre of the pattern rather than the fringe. So I would never allow any breezy evidence of this sort to blow my tables and calculations out of the window. Birds are not killed by bangs, and I have seen enough of the results of bad cartridges, both at the plate and in the field, to know that good patterns are indispensable for the best results, more especially for the longer reach.

Factors affecting pattern

The factors chiefly influencing patterns are the boring of the gun (not merely the degree of choke, but the whole of the boring, including the cone); the peak pressure of the cartridge; the velocity; the kind of wadding and turnover; the size and quality of the shot and the amount of deformation it suffers in being propelled from the gun. There are good grounds for believing that plated shot gives better patterns than plain, for the reasons explained in Chapter 7 (Cartridges), which amplifies several of these points.

Tightly bored and well choked guns exert the firmest control over pattern; but loosely bored and only slightly choked guns are capable of some of the best game-getting patterns, though they need more careful boring and regulating and greater care in the choice of cartridges. Especially do they need high-quality wadding and moderate velocity loads. High peak pressures and high velocity are usually bad for patterns, whatever the boring of the gun, though I would beware of being too categorical on this latter point (see Chapter 7). Large shot generally makes better quality, though, of necessity, thinner patterns than small.

The nature of the closure or turnover is important, the more so with open-bored guns. The crimp closure improves the percentage pattern which they throw by as much as 5 to 10 per cent, and eliminates the occasional "blown" or abnormally scattered pattern caused by the over-shot card interfering with the emerging pellets. The improvement is less marked with guns carrying more choke.

The modern plastic wad, incorporating a protective shot cup

which enfolds the charge during its passage up the bore, and so reduces the abrasion of the pellets by the barrel wall, tends to improve the quality and density of patterns, more especially from closely bored guns.

It also tends to increase the average energy of the pellets by reducing the number rendered comparatively ineffective through the loss by attrition of their original spherical form—and indeed of much of their substance.

Testing for pattern

It was a familiar article of faith with shooters in the muzzle-loading days that every gun had a load with which it shot best. This is equally true of modern breech-loaders, which can give widely different results, even with different brands of *good* cartridges. If therefore a shooter, and especially a comparative beginner, has confidence in his cartridges as suiting his gun, I would strongly recommend him to forget all about patterns and velocity and the like and to concentrate on shooting. He has much to lose and little to gain by worrying about these things. But if he strongly suspects his cartridges and cannot reasonably put the suspicion out of his mind, he should test his gun for pattern at the plate, and dispose of the matter one way or the other.

But the test *must* be properly carried out. It is worse than useless firing a single shot at a newspaper draped over a gate and from a distance that has not been accurately measured. Patterns are judged by firing not less than five shots from a previously fired barrel at a sheet of plain paper, or better, a whitewashed iron plate, at least four feet square, at a distance of 40 *measured yards* (not paces) from the shooter's position. The apparent centre of the pattern is selected by eye, and a 30-inch diameter circle described about it. The pattern enclosed in the circle is judged for uniformity, including freedom from undue central concentration. Any " balling ", or the sticking together of small clusters of pellets, is particularly noted as being a serious defect. The number of pellets inside the circle is then counted and noted. When this has been repeated for each shot, the average of the pellet-counts is taken and the percentage of the total pellets in

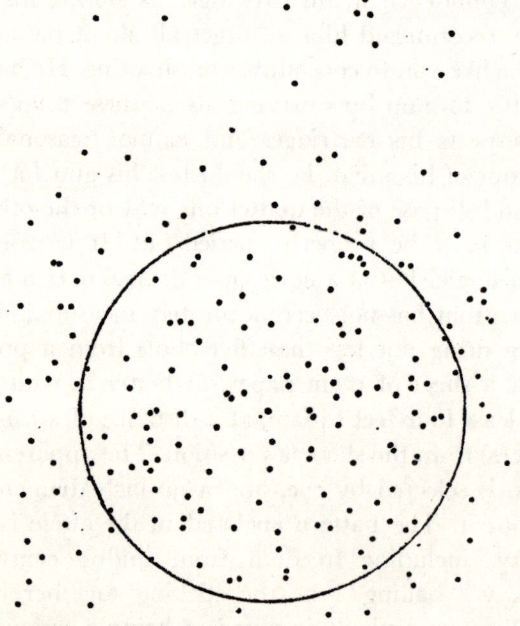

Fig. 9. 40-yard pattern, improved cylinder, $1\frac{1}{16}$ oz. No. 6 shot.

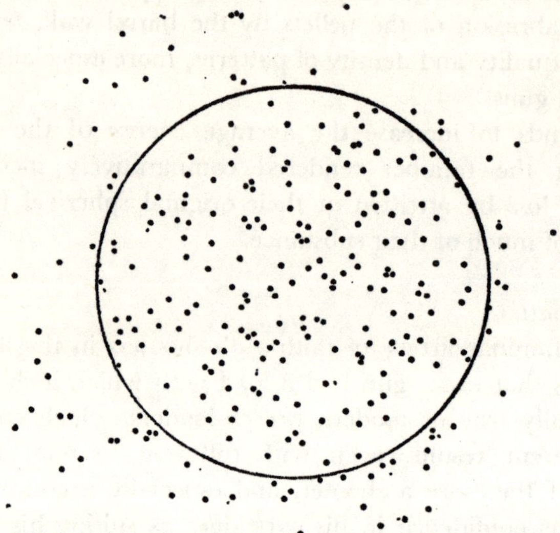

Fig. 10. 40-yard pattern, full choke $1\frac{1}{16}$ oz. No. 6 shot.

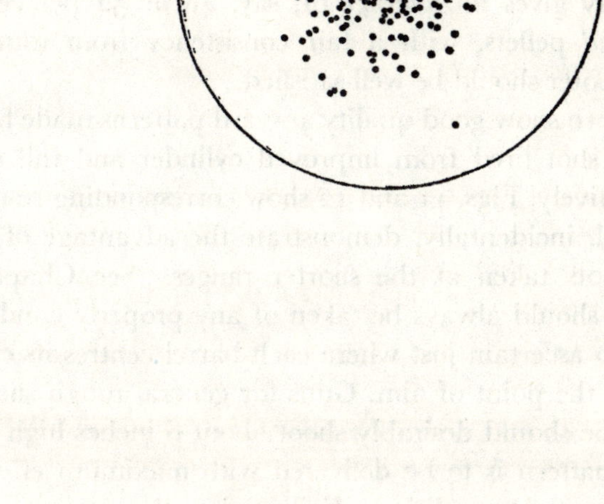

Fig. 11. 20-yard pattern, improved cylinder, $1\frac{1}{16}$ oz. No. 6 shot.

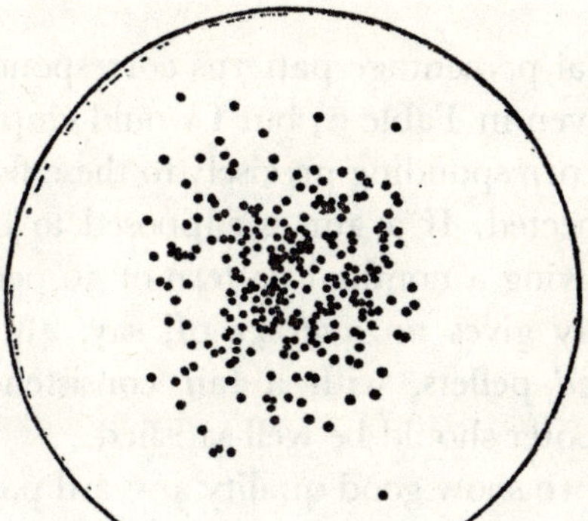

Fig. 12. 20-yard pattern, full choke, $1\frac{1}{16}$ oz. No. 6 shot.

the charge worked out. It is advisable to open one or two cartridges in the batch and check the number. Short weight is not unknown.

The nominal percentage patterns corresponding to the various borings are given in Table 2; but I would emphasise that average pellet-counts corresponding precisely to these figures are decidedly not to be expected. If a gun is supposed to be bored improved cylinder, throwing a nominal pattern of 50 per cent, at 40 yards, and it actually gives an average of, say, 48 or 52 per cent of *well-distributed* pellets, with a fair consistency from round to round, the shooter should be well satisfied.

Figs. 9 and 10 show good quality 40-yard patterns made by $1\frac{1}{16}$ oz. of No. 6 shot fired from improved cylinder and full choke barrels respectively. Figs. 11 and 12 show corresponding results at 20 yards, and, incidentally, demonstrate the advantage of open boring for shots taken at the shorter ranges. (See Chapter 6)

Advantage should always be taken of any properly conducted pattern test to ascertain just where each barrel centres its charge in relation to the point of aim. Guns for general rough shooting or driven game should desirably shoot about 6 inches high at 40 yards if the pattern is to be delivered with maximum effectiveness under practical conditions. Failing this, the gun may need re-fitting. (See Chapter 13)

An aspect of patterns neglected in this country arises from the fact that whereas shooting at distances beyond, say, 40 yards needs progressively more choke, shooting at distances below 30 yards often needs more open patterns than those thrown by a true cylinder. When shooting woodcock in covert, for example, many shots may have to be taken at 10 to 20 yards.

Continental sportsmen provide for such situations either by using "spreader" cartridges—that is, cartridges specially designed to give normal patterns at very short ranges, such as the F.N. "Dispersante" with its cubic shot—or by using guns rifled with a slow twist of about one turn in twelve feet.

Perhaps the most popular spreader cartridges are those in which the shot charge is divided lengthwise into four compartments by means of two interlocking rectangles of cardboard.

Rifled shot barrels are not available in this country, and if imported would appear to require a Firearm Certificate.

Some modern guns intended for skeet shooting have a kind of negative choke—an exaggerated conical or parallel enlargement of the bore at the muzzle which is claimed to improve the quality of patterns and possibly to increase their spread. Barrels so bored are sometimes described as "swamped" barrels.

CHAPTER SIX

CHOKE

CHOKE IS the name applied to a constriction at the muzzle end of the bore of a gun barrel whereby a portion of the emerging shot pellets are given an inward impulse, so that they spread less in the course of their flight, and make a smaller diameter pattern circle at a given distance than would otherwise be the case, and one that is therefore more densely garnished with shot.

There are two main kinds of choke as shown in fig. 14 (a) and (b). To these must be added the variable choke, described below. In the ordinary choke shown at (a) the bore diameter at the constriction is less than that at any other point. In the " recess " or " jug " choke shown at (b) the constriction comes at the end of a local enlargement and is not necessarily of smaller diameter than the rest of the bore. Recess choke has the advantage of being the only kind that can be *added*. It may thus be applied to restore some degree of choke to barrels that have lost what they originally had, through being shortened. It is, however, incapable of being used to introduce more than a slight degree of choke, and is more frequently used by the makers of good-class guns as a regulating device for adjusting patterns, in which case it may be associated with an ordinary choke.

The degree of choke carried by a barrel is expressed in several different ways, namely, (a) by a familiar system of terminology; (b) by the percentage pattern thrown; and (c) by the actual amount of the constriction, measured in thousandths of an inch, or " points ". If we put these three systems together, we get the following table.

TABLE 5. Definitions of Choke

(a) *Type of boring*	(b) *Percentage Pattern (in 30-inch circle at 40 yards)*	(c) *Approximate Points of Choke*
True Cyl.*	40	—
Imp. Cyl.	50	5
¼ Choke	55	10
½ Choke**	60	20
¾ Choke	65	30
Full Choke	70	40

(* Also known as " Skeet " or " Skeet No. 1 ")
(** ,, ,, ,, " Skeet No. 2 ")
(See Chapter 10 for Continental Choke markings)

An anomalous system

This system of definition is riddled with anomalies. For example, to obtain a full-choke pattern, one gunmaker may use 40 points of choke, but another (more probably nowadays) may use only 35. Again, a gun which gives a 70 per cent or full-choke pattern with 35 or 40 points of choke and a certain load or cartridge, may only give a 60 per cent pattern with another load or cartridge. To cut through these anomalies it is necessary to recognise that unless he is contemplating firing some kind of solid projectile, a shooter is not in the slightest degree interested in the amount of the constriction in the muzzle of his gun. I emphasise this because I have known one who felt deceived in respect of an allegedly fully choked gun when he found that the muzzle constriction was less than the 40 points he had expected. The actual constriction, then, is a design feature and is purely the gunmaker's concern. The shooter's concern is not the gun's design but its performance; and so, when discussing or specifying choke, it is best for him to define it by reference to the percentage pattern.

For the reasons already explained, however, the idea of percentage pattern must always be associated with the idea of a particular load or cartridge. If I am specifying the boring of a gun I always say that I want a *well-distributed* pattern of *about* 50 per cent (or whatever it may be) when using, say, the standard *Grand Prix* cartridge loaded with $1\frac{1}{16}$ oz. of a given size of shot and with a crimp closure.

The practical effect of choke from the ballistical point of view may be seen from Table 2, which I repeat here for convenience.

TABLE 2. Percentage Patterns for all Borings at all Ranges

Boring of Gun	*Range in yards* 30	35	40	45	50	55	60
True Cyl.	60	49	40	33	27	22	18
Imp. Cyl.	72	60	50	41	33	27	22
¼ Choke	77	65	55	46	38	30	25
½ Choke	83	71	60	50	41	33	27
¾ Choke	91	77	65	55	46	37	30
Full Choke	100	84	70	59	49	40	32

It will be recalled that in Chapter 4 the maximum effective range of a gun in relation to a given kind of game was defined as the greatest range at which it is reasonably certain that a clean kill will be made by a truly aimed shot; also, that this range was determined by the greatest distance to which the gun would throw the necessary minimum pattern. Referring to the above table, we see that the 40 per cent pattern thrown by a true cylinder at 40 yards is extended to over 45 yards by an improved cylinder; to 50 yards by a half choke and to 55 yards by a full choke. This then is the ballistical effect of choke—to extend the effective range of a gun.

TABLE 6. Diameter of Spread (being the diameter in inches covered by the bulk of the charge of a gun at various ranges for all calibres*)

Boring of Gun	*Range in yards* 10	15	20	25	30	35	40
True Cyl.	20	26	32	38	44	51	58
Imp. Cyl.	15	20	26	32	38	44	51
¼ Choke	13	18	23	29	35	41	48
½ Choke	12	16	21	26	32	38	45
¾ Choke	10	14	18	23	29	35	42
Full Choke	9	12	16	21	27	33	40

(**Special Note*: Because of the persistent fallacy that small-bore guns throw a smaller pattern circle than those of larger bore, it is necessary to emphasise that this is not the case. All bores throw approximately the same diameter circle, and the above table is therefore true for all calibres as stated—see fig. 15.)

But choke has other and no less practical effects. They arise from the reduced spread of the shot charge, the extent of which is apparent from the following table.

These figures repay careful study: they show that, at the ranges at which game is most frequently shot—probably between 25 and 35 yards—the diameter of spread, and therefore the margin available for covering the shooter's aiming errors, is much larger for the open borings than it is for the heavy chokes (see also figs. 9—12). This table and the preceding one furnish a joint explanation of the history of choke in the shooting field which it is instructive to examine.

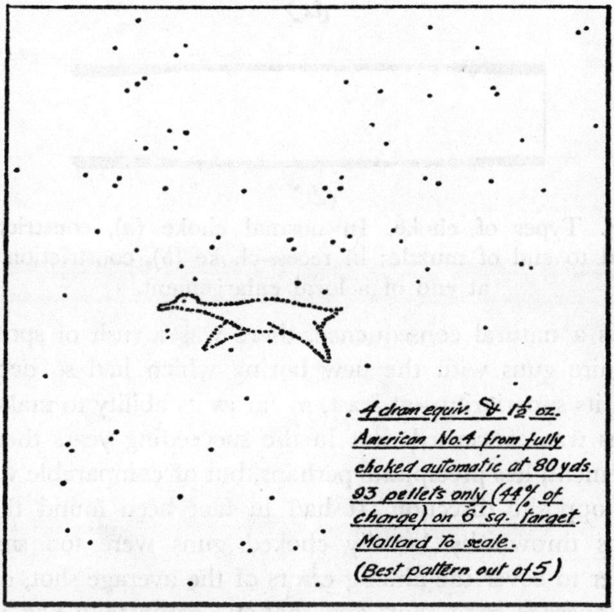

Fig. 13. 80-yard pattern made by 1½ oz. of American No. 4 shot (equivalent to English No. 3) from a fully-choked American automatic.

The verdict of a generation

On the strength of his British Patent No. 1501 of May 29, 1866, William Rochester Pape of Newcastle probably has the best claim to be regarded as the inventor of choke boring, though the practical development of the invention is justly credited to the famous Birmingham gunmaker, W. W. Greener. By 1874, he had so far perfected the art of boring guns in this way as to guarantee patterns of a closeness previously unknown. Indeed, his results attracted so much scepticism as to induce the *Field* to hold a grand trial in 1875, when the choke system thoroughly vindicated all the claims made on its behalf. It proved, in short, that it was capable of substantially extending the range of a

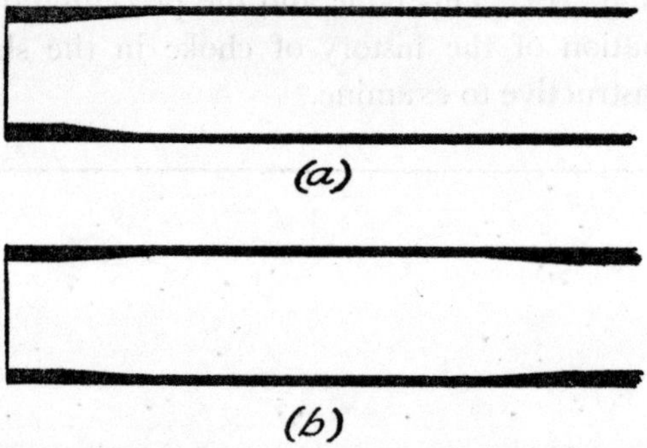

Fig. 14. Types of choke. In normal choke (*a*), constriction is confined to end of muzzle; in recess-choke (*b*), constriction comes at end of a local enlargement.

gun. As a natural consequence, there was a rush of sportsmen to acquire guns with the new boring which had so decisively proved its superiority—at least, so far as its ability to make close patterns was concerned. But in the succeeding years there was a movement, less precipitate perhaps, but of comparable volume, in the opposite direction. It had in fact been found that the patterns thrown by heavily choked guns were too small in diameter to cover the aiming errors of the average shot, or even of the average good shot, and that the game tally had usually suffered from the abandonment of the open boring. In consequence, the best boring for a game gun for the average man shooting in this country has long been recognised as improved cylinder for the right barrel and half to three-quarters choke for the left.

Nowadays we seem to be witnessing a double movement, both towards and away from choke boring. On the one hand,

Above : Barrel boring by the traditional, but still unsurpassed, spillboring process.
The boring bit is a straight square-section bar with one cutting edge, which is packed against the side of the bore by a wooden spill. Strips of paper, visible on the bench, are inserted between the spill and the boring bit according to the cut required.

Below : Machine-shop methods are used so far as possible to get down to the outside tolerances of actions and barrels. (Webley & Scott fully-machined action body for A. & D. boxlock gun)

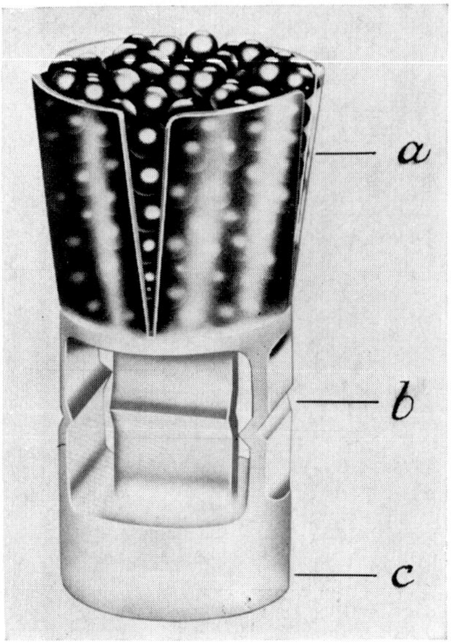

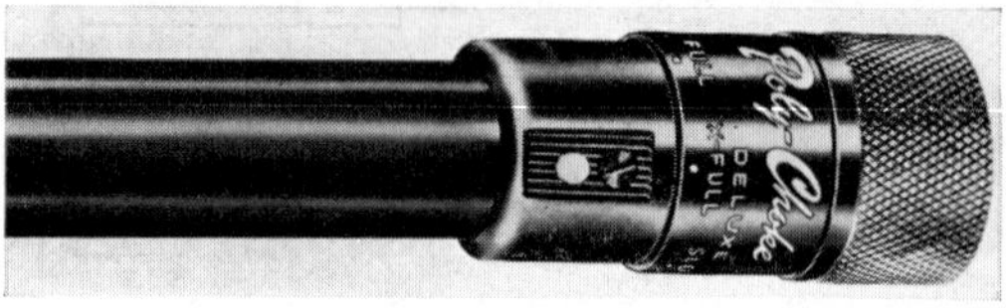

Above: A collet-type adjustable choke. These ingenious and attractive devices need expert fitting, and the careful checking of their performance

Left: A typical modern plastic wad, incorporating *a* a shot protector, *b* a collapsible portion for cushioning the initial rise of pressure of the powder gases, and *c* a cup-washer gas-seal

Below: The Winchester 'Winchoke'—a choke tube that is concealed inside the muzzle of the gun

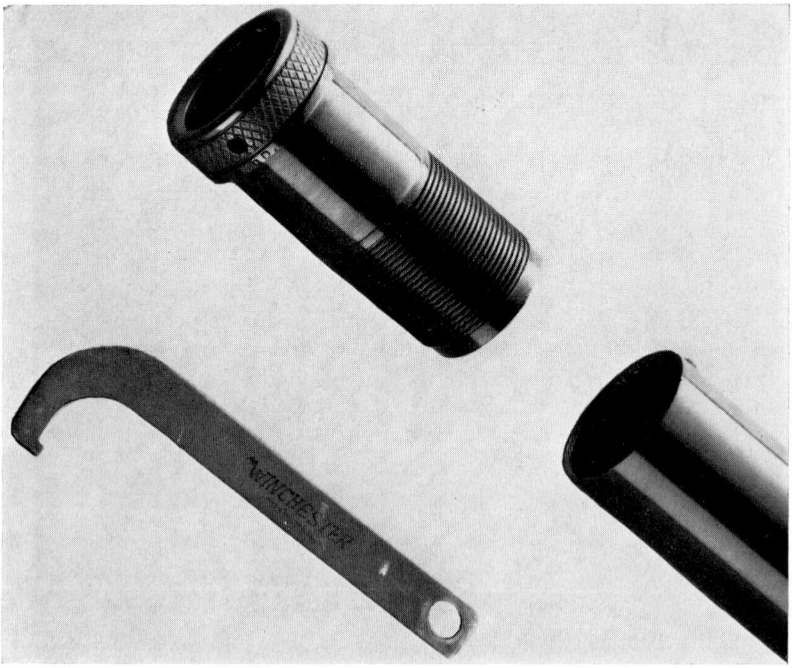

many newcomers to shooting, and most uncritical shooters buying guns in the popular-price class, are buying the heavily choked variety, mostly of foreign origin. On the other hand, considerable numbers of the more knowledgeable ones, headed by the skeet shooters, are rediscovering the virtues of open boring. The former class—the new class of patrons of the full choke—adopt this boring for a variety of reasons, chiefly because they consider

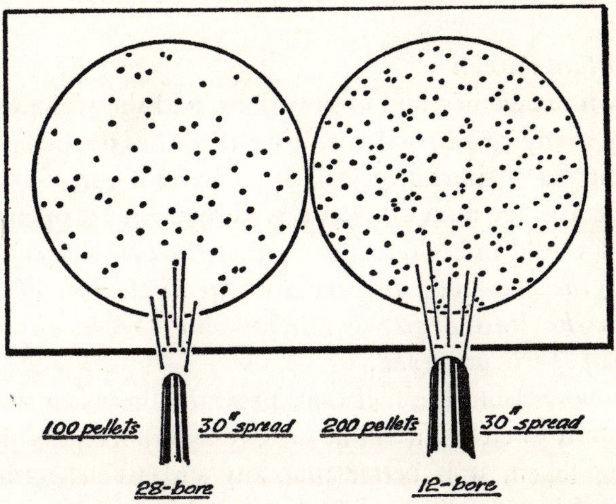

Fig. 15. Small and large bores give the same spread.

it more suitable for pigeon shooting and wildfowling, but partly, I have no doubt, because of its psychological appeal and for no better reason than that that happens to be the boring of guns offered to them in the shops.

Considering that a whole generation of shooters, after having eagerly taken to heavily choked guns, turned away from them, chastened and disillusioned, it may well be asked why do so many foreign and American gunmakers still send their guns out with this kind of boring? There are two simple reasons—choke can easily be removed if it is not wanted; and on those occasions when a fully choked gun is held really straight on a distant quarry, the result is likely to give the shooter a good impression of his weapon, and to divert all blame for frequent misses to himself. He is unlikely to lump the gun and himself together as an inefficient combination, and in the absence of any capacity for self-improvement, to blame the gun as the defaulting partner. Yet, all too frequently, that is what he should do.

Another thing he should do is to take a note of the modern, crimp-closed cartridge as a significant development in this context. Not only do open-bored guns show a 5 to 10 per cent improvement in pellet-count when using these cartridges, but they are also free from the old reproach of "blown" patterns.

An important maxim

My own experience and observations, and the views expressed to me by many correspondents, leave me in no doubt that unless the conditions of sport imperatively demand a gun of maximum range, the average man is better served by the more open borings. Indeed, I would unhesitatingly say that *the best degree of choke for filling the game bag and avoiding the displeasure of the cook is always the least degree consistent with the requirements of the class of sport concerned.*

This follows from the fact that, provided there is a sufficiently close pattern to ensure a kill at the average range at which birds are being taken, it is better that any surplus pellets available should be devoted to increasing the spread rather than increasing the already adequate density. Thereby hits are scored which might otherwise be misses.

A good idea of the relationship between choke and personal aiming error may be obtained by loading a familiar gun with dummy cartridges or "snap-caps" and taking snap shots at a target as in fig. 16. The shooter should face the target at the stated distance; then close the eyes and turn right round. Then open the eyes and fire at the aiming mark as quickly as possible without fluster, pulling the trigger just as the gun comes into the shoulder and "calling" the shot—that is, mentally photographing the position of the foresight at the click of the hammer. Shots falling as at *A* would be misses both with an improved cylinder and with a full choke barrel. Shots as at *B* would be misses with the choke but hits with the cylinder; and only those as at *C* would be hits with the full choke. The *B* shots are obviously the significant ones. If you repeat this practice several

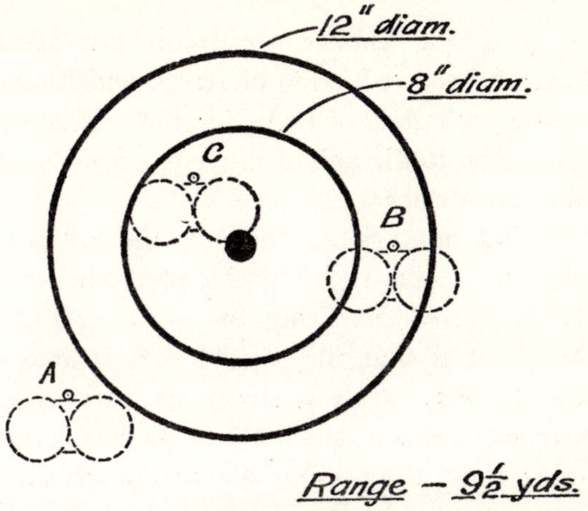

Fig. 16. Aiming target for demonstrating difference between spread of full choke and improved cylinder boring. (Equivalent to 25 yards actual range.)

times on successive days and keep a record of your scores, you will have a fair idea of the possible significance of spread in your particular case.

Variable chokes

These comparatively modern devices, adaptable to all single-barrelled weapons, take three forms. The first comprises a short extension screwed on to the barrel and incorporating a plain choke as illustrated in fig. 14 (*a*). It is usual for the sportsman to have a set of these extensions, each incorporating a choke of different degree.

The second kind, unlike the first, is truly variable. It is sometimes called a collet choke, after a kind of mechanic's chuck which it resembles, and comprises a constriction divided by longitudinal cuts into a number of fingers, rather like the petals of a closed flower. These fingers are held together at their outer ends by a conical ring which may be screwed in or out, thus squeezing or releasing them and varying the amount of the constriction. The screw ring has a clicking mechanism and is marked on its outside so that the degree of choke may be identified.

Both the foregoing chokes are frequently associated with a muzzle-brake for the reduction of recoil, which takes the form of a short tube with slots or holes for the release of propellent gases at right angles to the axis of the bore. (See Chapter 9 for an explanation of this device.)

The third kind of variable choke is the automatic variety, which consists of a collet-type variable choke in which the controlling ring is shifted on firing by a spring-opposed inertia weight. The effect is that the second shot is fired to a closer pattern than the first—truly a strenuous attempt to repeat in a single-barrelled weapon an inherent facility of the double.

Examples of these three kinds of variable choke are (1) the Cutts Compensator; (2) the Poly-choke and (3) the Adjustomatic. This last has an integral muzzle-brake.

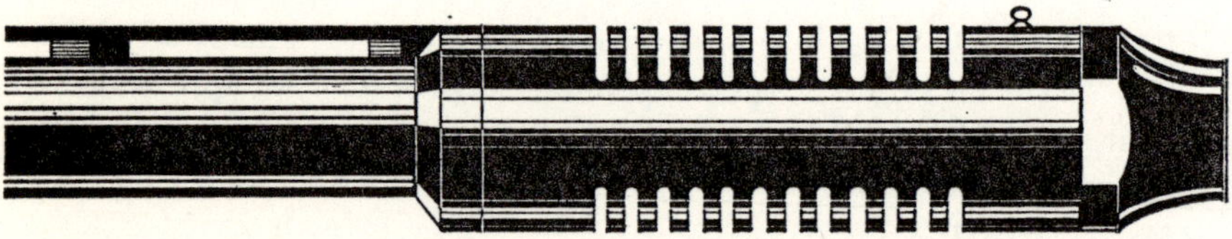

Fig. 17. The Cutts Compensator with short choke tube attached. For principle of action see Fig. 22.

As a means for adding flexibility to single-barrelled weapons, these devices are attractive, but they all, in varying degrees, involve hanging extra weight on to a gun at the very place from which gunsmiths have laboured for a century and a half to remove it. The automatic chokes are particularly bad in this respect, weighing, as they may, as much as six ounces, and adding possibly .05 *g* units (see Chapter 12) to the moment of inertia of a gun.

The collet-type adjustable chokes are especially disappointing. Despite their convenience, they cannot normally be relied on to give consistent patterns of the density conforming to the indications of the setting. The performance of these devices should therefore never be taken for granted.

It should be noted that variable chokes, being larger in diameter than the barrels to which they are fitted, depress the bore axis in relation to the line of aim. (The only known exception to this is the Winchester " Winchoke "—a replaceable choke tube that screws *inside* the muzzle of the gun.) They also tend to increase the negative " flip " of the barrel on firing, so that their overall effect is normally to cause the gun to shoot low. To correct this fault, so damaging to performance, the firms that fit these devices usually give the barrel, or the ventilated portion of the attachment, a slight and scarcely perceptible upward set. The fitting of these chokes and the correction of the shooting is thus a matter for a skilled gunsmith accustomed to the work.

CHAPTER SEVEN

CARTRIDGES

Modern British cartridges for game, wildfowl and clay target shooting range from the $3\frac{1}{4}$-inch 8-gauge loaded with 2 oz. of shot to the 2-inch .410 with five-sixteenths. Notable recent newcomers are the two Eley 12-gauge magnums—the $2\frac{3}{4}$-inch loaded with $1\frac{1}{2}$ oz. and the 3-inch loaded with $1\frac{5}{8}$.

The standard Eley $2\frac{1}{2}$-inch, 12-gauge game cartridge is a waterproof cartridge with a crimp-closed, polyethylene case, a non-corrosive cap and a vegetable felt wad, throwing a charge of $1\frac{1}{16}$ oz. of medium shot to an average or "observed" velocity, measured over the first 20 yards of flight, of about 1,070 feet per second, corresponding to a muzzle velocity of, say, 1,320.

At the time of writing, paper-cased cartridges are still available in several British-made and imported varieties, and are preferred by some shooters who believe that they give more regular ballistics. There is some *prima facie* reason for this belief, but, although it is probably true, I have no supporting evidence. They are also free from some curious contamination phenomena* that have been observed, chiefly in America, and are not yet fully explained.

The cartridge case. The case has at least three functions—(a) it has to act as a container, preferably waterproof, for the components of the charge, including the cap; (b) it has to restrain the emergence of the shot until the powder is properly ignited; and (c) it has to seal the breech against the pressure of propellent gases. Of these three functions, the last is unquestionably the most important. Apart from the screw plug, no mechani-

* See "Cartridge Chamber Contamination" by Gough Thomas—*Shooting Times & Country Magazine*, March 15th, 1969

cal device ever succeeded in efficiently sealing small-arms at the breech until the elastic cartridge case was invented. Breech loaders with hand-fitted, inelastic metal cartridges have been known for centuries. Henry VIII had such a weapon, which may still be seen at the Tower of London. But the simple idea of a cartridge case which was sufficiently elastic to expand and fill the chamber as the gas pressure rose inside it, and thus to seal the junction between chamber and breech, even in the absence of any accurate fitting of the mechanical parts, was slow to arrive. It was the elastic, breech-sealing, pin-fire cartridge, invented by Houiller in the 1840s and adopted by Lefaucheux, which more than anything else ensured the success of the drop-down breech loader that bears the latter's name—the first modern sporting gun.

It will be obvious that the use of paper for cartridge cases is an economic compromise. The case should be waterproof, but paper is not. Nor is it sufficiently elastic under certain conditions. The chief defects of paper are that when it becomes damp it swells and may cause the cartridges to jam in the gun, particularly if it is a self-loader; and that if it becomes abnormally dry and thereby loses elasticity, it is prone to split. In extreme cases, this may cause " cut-offs ", when the body of the case becomes completely detached from the head. For this and other reasons paper cartridges should never be stored in excessively warm and dry situations, such as airing cupboards, nor should they be left for long in closed motor cars exposed to the hot sun. They are best stored under the ordinary, temperate, indoor conditions to be found in dry houses in this country.

But despite the disadvantages of paper cases, they have served shooters well for over a century, and with commonsense and by no means onerous precautions, are as nearly as possible trouble-free. It is not surprising that some ammunition manufacturers and shooters still pin their faith to them. Perhaps the greater reloading potential of plastic cases is their only important advantage to trap and skeet shooters.

As stated in Chapter 5 (Patterns), the closure of the case by crimping instead of by using a cardboard top-wad has a beneficial effect on patterns.

Length of case. Cartridges were hitherto denoted by the length of the unloaded case, which was never greater than the length of the chamber. Since crimp closures became the rule, they have been denoted by the minimum length of the chamber for which they are designed, as stated on the carton. *They must never be used in chambers of any lesser length.*

Powders. Modern powders are "double-based" (i.e. nitroglycerine and gelatinised or fibrous nitro-cellulose) compounds. Progress latterly has been chiefly in the direction of improving the consistency of their performance and in their stability with age and under widely varying conditions of storage, which, as an eminent specialist complained to me, may be anything between the equator and the poles, or between the bread-oven and the shed at the bottom of the garden. Notable progress has also been made in improving the controls regulating the rate of burning. For example, I.C.I. now have no less than seven grades of their Nobel-Glasgow powder available, ranging from the fastest-burning sort normally required for driving light charges of shot at high velocity, to the slowest-burning or progressive kinds required for magnum loads, including that of the 3-inch .410. We shall need to return to these graded characteristics of modern powders when considering loads.

The cap. Intimately connected with the powder is the cap or primer. For the best results, it must be adapted to match the powder, the various kinds of which vary in their ignitibility. The modern non-corrosive or styphnate cap is a great advance over the highly corrosive caps of the past. Used in conjunction with a suitable powder, it eliminates the bugbear of barrel corrosion, and has largely reduced the business of gun-cleaning to that of merely preventing common atmospheric rusting. Further, unlike earlier caps, its correct functioning is independent of the quality of the striker blow; if it goes off, it goes off properly.

Wadding. The wad has a vital function to perform in the cartridge. It has to seal the bore, and to confine the white-hot, high-pressure, propellent gases to the space behind the shot-charge. Any leakage of gas among the pellets is highly detrimental to patterns and may result in clusters of them becoming fused together, or "balling"—a dangerous thing, for such a cluster is capable of travelling far beyond ordinary shot and inflicting injury on someone who might be considered well out of range.

The sealing-power, or obturating-power as it is called, of a wad is dependent on its elasticity and its ability to translate the powerful thrust of the powder gases into a lateral thrust against the sides of the bore. Best quality, greased, white felt is one of the most efficient wadding materials ever known, but it has the drawback of being expensive. Brown felt can be good, but it lacks the uniformity necessary for regular ballistics. A great variety of other material has been tried, notably cork, but cork lowers ballistics and has the peculiar disadvantage of accepting a high degree of longitudinal compression without developing any corresponding lateral thrust. It is, in fact, a poor obturator, as may be seen by putting a felt wad and cork wad side by side in a vice and squeezing them up together. By the time they are compressed to half their original length, the felt wad will have spread out greatly in diameter but the cork wad hardly at all.

Apart from simple materials, many composite wads have been developed. Among those that have survived, cork and felt appear to be the favourite components.

By far the most popular wad in this country in recent years has been the "Kleena" wad, developed by I.M.I. This is a vegetable felt originally made of sugar-cane fibre. It is claimed to have the merit of consistency and to prevent the leading of the bores.

The plastic wad, incorporating a protective shot cup, as described in Chapter 5 (Patterns) is now being introduced in certain Eley cartridges, and its use will almost certainly be extended.

Shot. Shot is mostly of the so-called "chilled" variety, which is harder than pure lead. It is actually a lead-arsenic-antimony alloy, and in the ordinary sizes is usually made by dropping molten lead from a kind of sieve at the top of a high tower. The molten drops of lead form more or less perfect globules as they fall, and the height of the drop is sufficient to give them time to solidify before they reach the tank of water at the bottom of the tower. Shot is also made by machine, when it is claimed to be more uniform and more truly spherical, though there is some doubt of its superiority over the best dropped variety.

If a gun is to shoot at its best, it must be loaded with best-quality shot, that is, shot that is as nearly as possible perfectly round, and of uniform size and density. For the improvement of patterns, the very best shot is nowadays plated with copper or nickel. This has the effect of inhibiting the "cold-welding" or sticking together of the pellets, whereby strings and clusters of

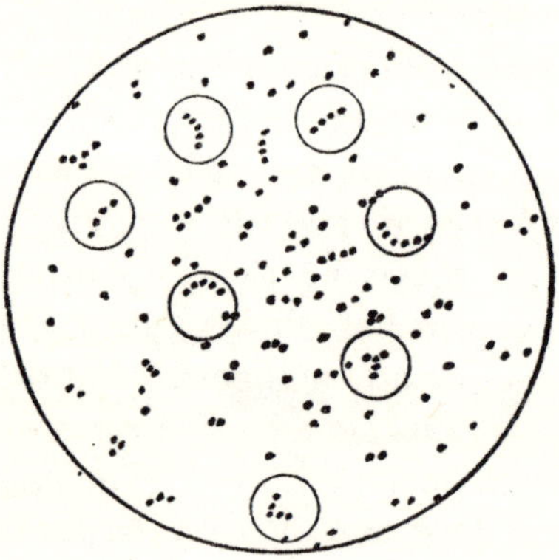

Fig. 18. Cold welding of shot pellets. Existence of local strings and clusters of pellets in pattern diagrams, as in small circles, indicates cohesion through cold welding over part of their course.

them may fly together over part of their course, giving a certain characteristic defect in patterns chiefly recognisable in those thrown by high pressured cartridges. (See fig. 18)

Cartridge manufacture. In recent years improvements in factory-loaded cartridges have been responsible for a big reduction in the amount of loading undertaken by individual gunmakers. These improvements are not merely those attributable to better and more uniform components, but to refinements in production technique. Chief among these are a scientific sampling and continuous testing of finished cartridges for pressure and velocity, whereby deviations from established standards, such as those that might be caused by slight variations in powder from batch to batch, are at once detected and corrected or compensated. To these measures must be added visual inspection at each appropriate stage as well as X-ray inspection of the finished product, all of which have been responsible for some impressive attainments in consistency as well as quality of performance.

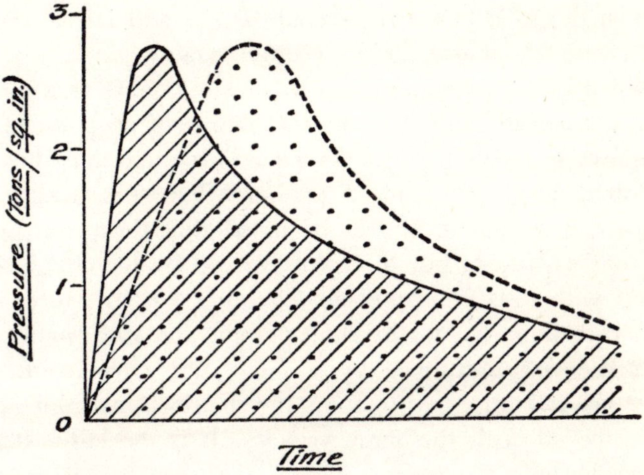

Fig. 19. Effect of progressive powders. Solid curve is pressure curve of normal powder; dotted curve that of progressive powder. In the case of the latter, pressure rises more slowly and is more sustained, but peak shows no increase.

Loads (*general*). For many years our loads were more or less standardised. They had been arrived at by fully two centuries of experience, which had taught us the charges of shot required to deal effectively with the various kinds of game met with in this country and the best-sized bores from which to fire them. For example, the standard load for general game shooting was $1\frac{1}{16}$ oz., which might be reduced to 1 oz. or increased to $1\frac{1}{8}$ oz. according to circumstances and the taste and fancy of the shooter. For pigeon shooting (meaning, originally, live pigeon shooting from traps) we used $1\frac{1}{4}$ oz.; and for wildfowling $1\frac{3}{8}$ oz. These loads have been found to go best in $2\frac{1}{2}$-inch, $2\frac{3}{4}$-inch and 3-inch 12-bores respectively. Larger and smaller loads had similarly been arrived at for other kinds and conditions of shooting, ranging from the 3 oz. allotted to the 4-bore to the $\frac{9}{16}$ oz. assigned to the 28-bore.

But in recent years, a range of slow-burning or progressive powders has become available, enabling larger charges of shot to be handled by a given bore without increasing the peak pressure. The way these powders work may be seen from fig. 19, in which the solid curve represents the rise and fall of pressure with a normal powder when plotted against time. The area enclosed by the curve, indicated by cross-hatching, is a measure of the *momentum* imparted to the charge of shot. Now, with a progressive powder, we might get a curve like that shown by the dotted line, indicating a pressure that rises more slowly but is more sustained. It will be noted that the peak pressure is $2\frac{3}{4}$ tons as before; but the area enclosed by the curve, shown stippled with dots, is appreciably greater. So, therefore, is the momentum imparted to the shot charge; and since momentum equals *Weight** multiplied by *Velocity*, the effect could be a greater velocity imparted to the same shot load, or a larger shot load propelled with the same velocity. It is the latter that we are considering.

This process of increasing the weight of shot that can be handled by a given gun without increasing the peak pressure is useful in enabling a larger load to be used to meet the needs of a special occasion, for the sake of which the extra recoil may be tolerated. A good example is that provided by the I.M.I. *Maximum* cartridge loaded with $1\frac{3}{16}$ oz. of shot, but suitable for firing in an ordinary $2\frac{1}{2}$-inch chambered 12-bore normally used with $1\frac{1}{16}$ oz. But things have gone much further than that, particularly in America, where 3-inch, 20-bore magnum cartridges are now being loaded with as much as $1\frac{1}{8}$ oz. of shot and corresponding 12-bores with $1\frac{7}{8}$. As I am dealing separately with the magnum principle in Chapter 11, I am only concerned

* I have used the expression "weight" instead of "mass" herein as being more generally comprehensible, though less correct scientifically

here with the cartridge aspect of these heavy American loads. Some of them set up working pressures substantially in excess of those for which our guns are designed, and should not be used without consulting the makers of the gun in question as to their suitability. In any event they may cause excessive recoil unless used in guns of appropriate weight, or in a type of self-loading weapon which reduces the recoil otherwise felt by the shooter.

But apart from these considerations, many shooters who take to these heavy loads are disappointed with them. The reason, I have no doubt, is that they expect too much of them. They fail to recognise sufficiently clearly that the shotgun is fundamentally a short-range weapon, and that nothing can make it otherwise. They accept, say, 50 yards as their greatest possible reach with a standard, $1\frac{1}{16}$ oz. load; but when they adopt a " Maximum " cartridge, loaded, perhaps, with a modest $1\frac{3}{16}$ oz., they expect a disproportionate increase in range, and are quite likely to fire at birds 60 to 70 yards away. Disappointment is inevitable: their increased load has not increased their effective range to any appreciable extent, as a study of the diagram on page 47 should make clear.

Standard loads. The standard loads for the more popular gauges using Nobel-Glasgow powders are set out in Chapter 8 (Home-loading and Reloading).

High-velocity loads. As applied to shotgun cartridges, " high-velocity " is an inexact term. At one extreme, it can be nothing more than an advertising slogan, applied to a cartridge giving an observed velocity, as defined on page 70, of perhaps 1,050 feet per second, corresponding to a muzzle velocity of, say, 1,270; and at the other to a really high-velocity cartridge giving corresponding figures of 1,150 and 1,475, these latter being about the highest practicable values for medium shot.

Fig. 20 gives a graphic comparison between two such cartridges. The two curves show the respective velocities at all points of the range with No. 6 shot, and the relative figures of muzzle velocity, striking velocity and energy at 50 yards. It will be seen that, for the $9\frac{1}{2}$ per cent increase in observed velocity there is a 16 per cent increase in muzzle velocity and therefore in recoil; but only a 7 per cent gain in the striking velocity at 50 yards. Owing, however, to the fact that energy is proportional to the square of the velocity, the gain in energy at this range is 14 per cent. Most high-velocity cartridges, as sold, would show a good deal smaller gain than in this somewhat extreme case.

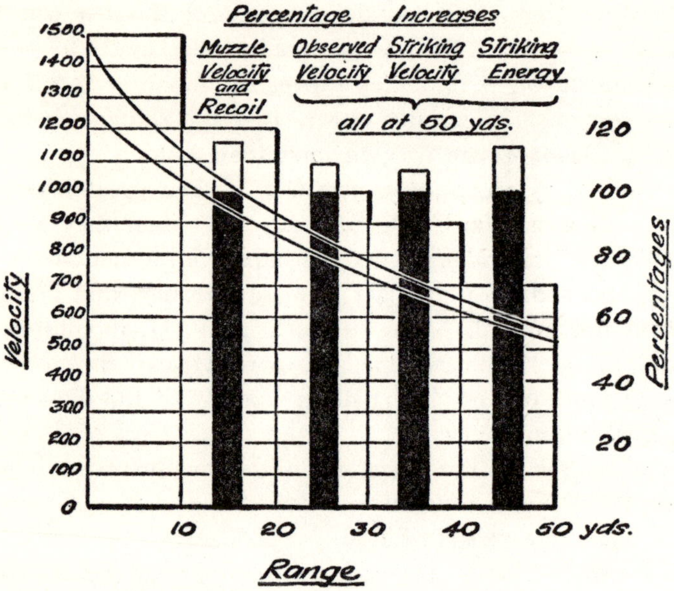

Fig. 20. High-velocity and normal cartridges compared.

Since, as I have already explained, patterns normally fail before velocity, I have some difficulty in attaching solid advantages to high-velocity loads, more especially as they tend to impair patterns, particularly those thrown by open-bored guns. I have indeed seen some deplorable results with this combination.

Nevertheless, some eminent manufacturers claim that with the right powder, careful loading and the right gun, pattern quality *can* be preserved, when a high-velocity load may possibly justify the use of smaller shot, thus maintaining adequate pattern density and pellet energy at a longer range than normal; but, for my own part, I would by no means take the fulfilment of these prerequisite conditions for granted: I would not be prepared to accept a substantial increase in recoil for an advantage that the pattern plate might well prove to be evanescent. The wildfowler in particular, with his relatively large shot, must seek range in the various means for maintaining pattern density rather than in any enhancement of normal velocities.

New developments. Although, for the economic and other reasons already indicated, the paper-cased cartridge is likely to be with us for a long time yet, the trend of modern developments may repay brief consideration.

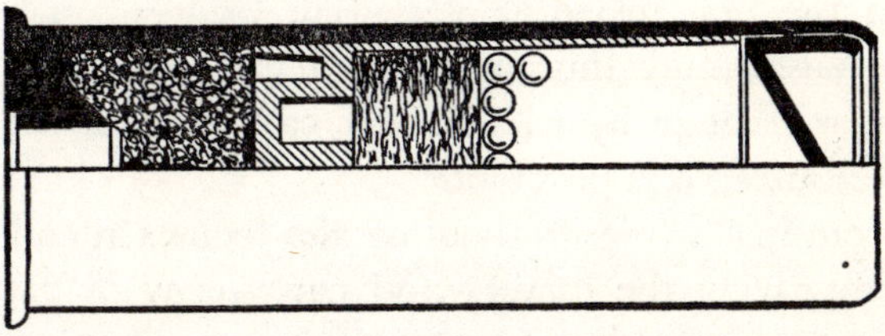

Fig. 21. The Wanda Cartridge. Half-section showing the one-piece polycarbonate case and special plastic top wad. The over-powder wad is an Alcan "Flite-max"—a combination plastic and fibre wad incorporating a protective shot cup.

The plastic case shows every indication of remaining the normal standard case of the future. Improvements are likely to take place chiefly in the field of manufacturing technique, and possibly in the use of alternative or modified materials.

Two cartridges already on the market exemplify these trends. The first is the Winchester "compression-formed" cartridge shown facing page 80. This has a polyethylene case made in one piece by an ingenious process in the course of which the molecular structure of the material is so modified as greatly to increase its tensile strength. The metal head could probably be dispensed with in conventional guns, but is retained out of consideration for the severe duty imposed on the rim by the claw-type extractors of repeaters.

The Wanda cartridge (fig. 21), made by the Wanda Cartridge

Company of Houston, Texas, breaks new ground by using a straight injection moulding of polycarbonate plastic. The natural strength of this material, which, incidentally, is transparent, enables the metal head to be dispensed with, but makes it impracticable to use a turnover or crimp to seal the case, which is therefore closed by a specially shaped plastic plug or top-wad. It is claimed that this closure device does not interfere with patterns.

The ever-rising cost of cartridges, combined with the growing popularity of clay pigeon shooting, will undoubtedly increase interest in home-loading, hitherto relatively neglected in this country; and this in turn will place a premium on the cartridge case with the best reloading potential. Conventional crimp or rolled turnovers may thus be marked for extinction, as in the Wanda case, though by what means cannot at present be foreseen. There are several possibilities.

The boom in clay pigeon shooting also focuses attention on any way of improving the quality and consistency of patterns and shortening the shot-string. One of the means to this end is shot of the highest possible degree of uniformity and of the utmost resistance to deformation in its course up the barrel. We already have machine-made shot and shot plated with resistant metals, and the scope for future improvement would appear to lie chiefly in reducing the cost of these refinements.

Another possibility I have suggested* is that the advent of the plastic case with skived mouth and plastic wad might justify the abolition of the chamber cone and the re-introduction of the chamberless gun, as designed for use with the old, all-metal " Perfect " cases, now no longer made. The abolition of the cone should help to reduce pellet-deformation, and would confer some incidental advantages. This suggestion could well form the subject of further experiments.

The serious amount of lead-poisoning among wildfowl in America, due to their picking up lead pellets on heavily shot-over marshes, is directing attention there to the use of non-toxic

* " Doing Away with the Cone ", by Gough Thomas—*Shooting Times & Country Magazine*—July 20th, 1968, and " Case Non-Proven "—May 3rd, 1969

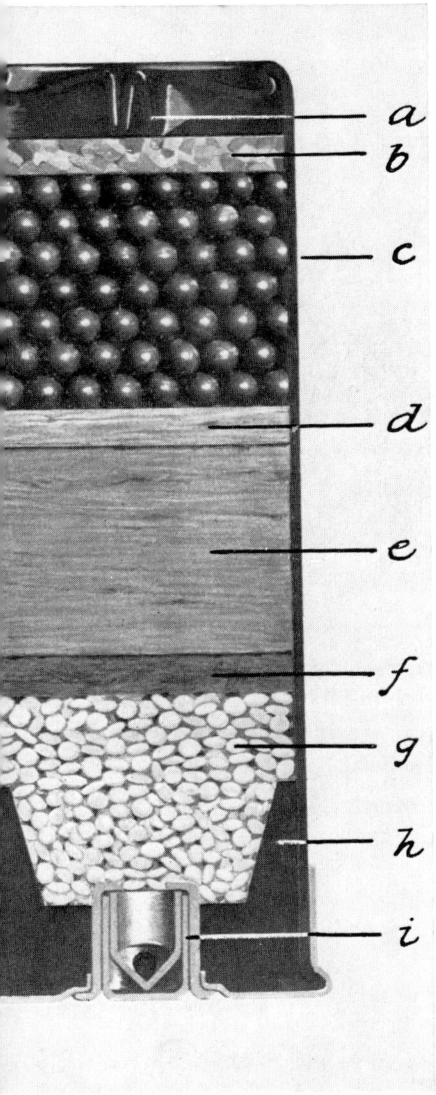

A modern Eley cartridge, showing *a* crimp closure, *b* frangible waterproof seal, *c* plastic case, *d* under-shot card, *e* vegetable felt 'Kleena' wad, *f* over powder card, *g* double-based powder, *h* compressed paper base-wad, and *i* cap or primer

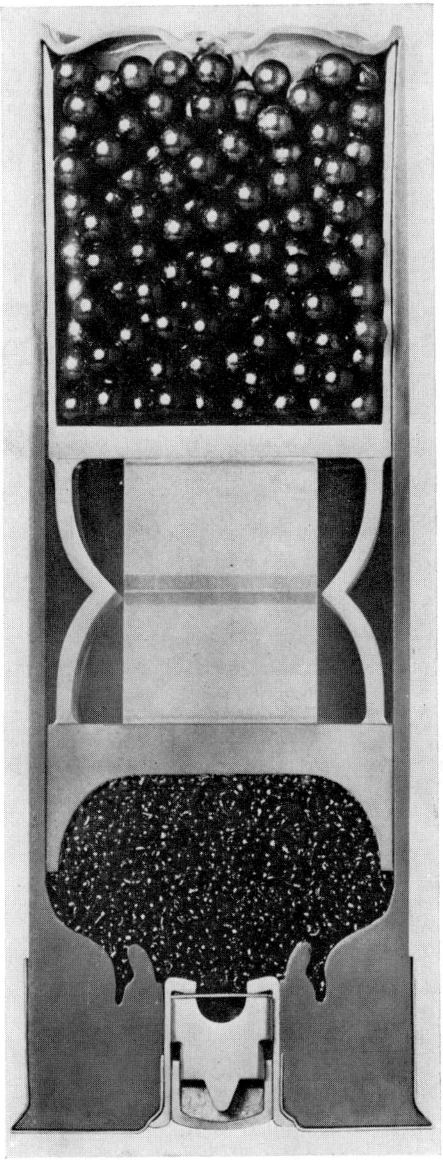

The Winchester compression-formed cartridge. The case of this cartridge is formed from a solid slug of polyethylene plastic and by a process that greatly increases the strength of the material

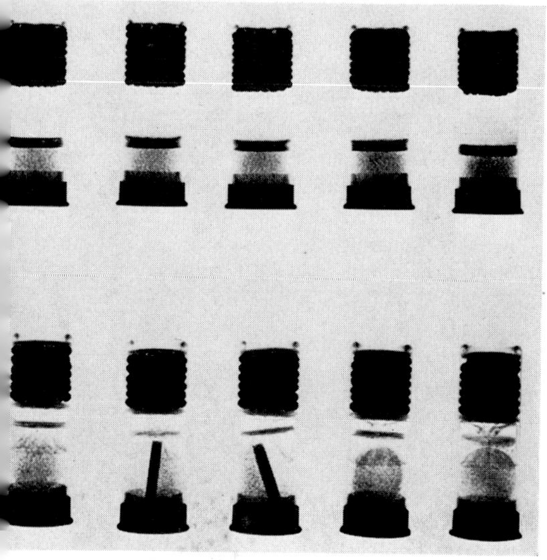

X-rayed cartridges: upper row correct, lower row defective (IMI)

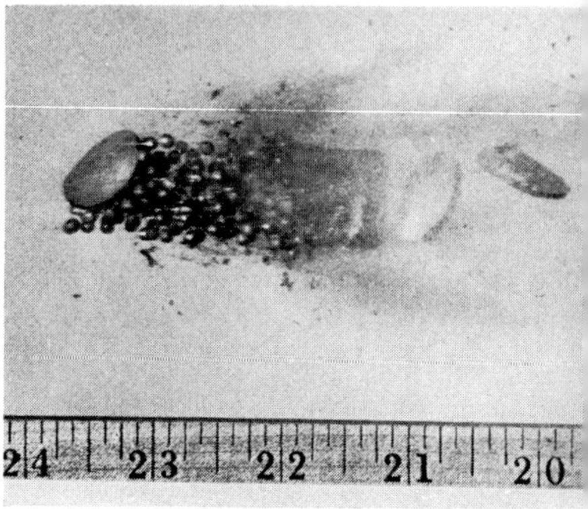

A shot charge in flight two feet from the muzzle, showing interference of the top wad with the development of the pattern

Testing Eley cartridges for pressure, velocity and recoil in a pendulum gun. The counter chronographs on the left indicate time up the barrel, and time of flight

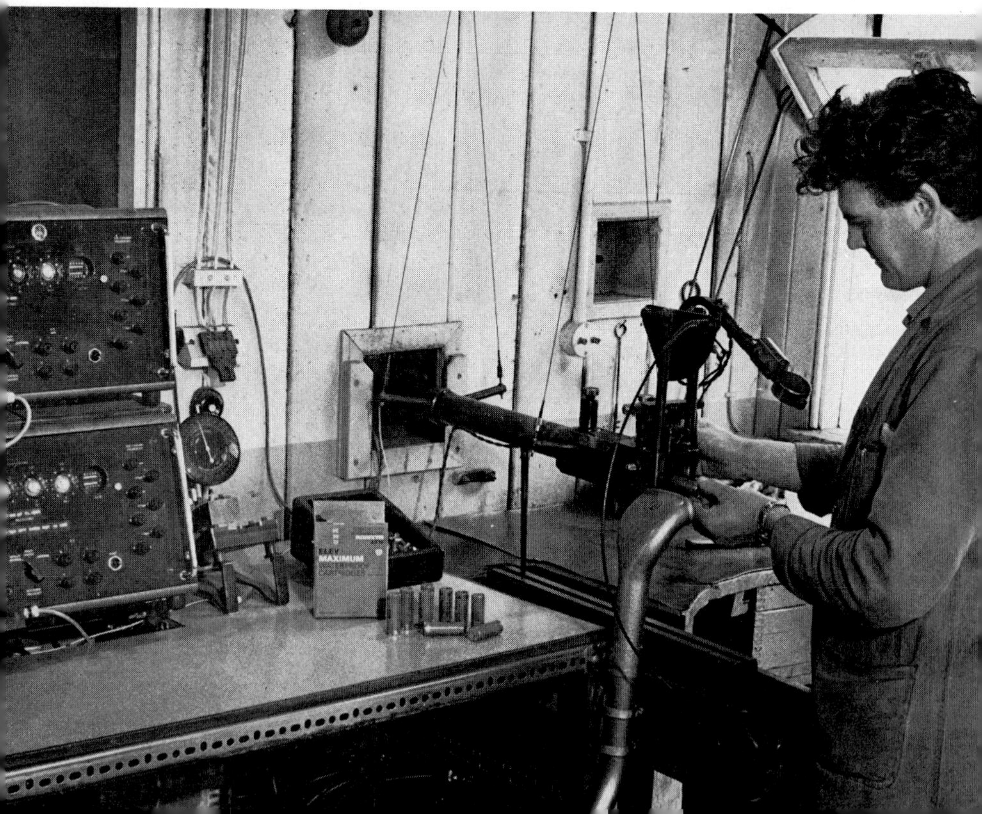

shot. Of the many ingenious things contemplated to this end, soft iron shot appears to be the most feasible; and although its use imposes limitations on the range and power of guns, and gives rise to several incidental problems affecting them, we are likely to hear more of it. Iron-shotted Eley or Kynoch cartridges were, in fact, produced and marketed in this country during the First World War.

Imported cartridges—a warning. The pressures developed by British cartridges are regulated to conform to the appropriate standards of British proof, which in turn have been laid down in due relation to the guns and loads evolved by our home gun trade to meet the needs and preferences of British sportsmen. But this is not the case with some imported cartridges, which the prudent user will therefore avoid unless they are offered with explicit assurance (preferably printed on the carton) as to their suitability for use in British guns of clearly defined proof status.

CHAPTER EIGHT

HOME-LOADING AND RELOADING

IN THE early days of breechloaders it was commonly assumed that the sportsman would need or wish to load his own cartridges, and guns were often sent out with the necessary equipment in the case. It comprised dippers for powder and shot, a combined de-capper and re-capper, a hand-rammer and a turnover machine. By these simple means, satisfactory black powder cartridges could be turned out.

When the breechloader had become thoroughly established, practically every gunsmith loaded cartridges on his premises, if necessary according to the individual requirements of his customers. At the same time, many shooters continued to load their own.

But the advent of smokeless powder and the rise of the big sporting ammunition manufacturers produced a change in this situation. The new powder was more tricky to load—no longer could it be safely entrusted to an apprentice or undertaken by a slapdash amateur. Accordingly, many sportsmen gave up home-loading.

So did many gunsmiths, who found it paid them to let the big manufacturers load their cartridges—still bearing the gunsmith's name and brand, but probably of better and more uniform quality than he himself had ever produced.

Things progressed in this way until the end of the last war, when the boom in clay pigeon shooting, and the American influence that accompanied it, brought about a sharp revival of interest in home-loading. There was also an economic urge. Cartridge prices had risen steeply and were continuing to rise, and clay pigeon shooters had great appetites for ammunition.

Besides, new and improved loading equipment—mostly American—was coming on to the market. And so the present home-loading revival set in, and has since prospered. In addition to providing a source of economical practice ammunition, many have found that home-loading becomes an interesting and self-justifying hobby. Any intelligent person, with the equipment and components now available, can turn out safe and satisfactory shotgun ammunition, provided that he carefully and consistently follows the instructions freely available.

Precautions. Cartridge loading requires a place where all equipment and components can be set up or set out in familiar order, and where the work can proceed without interruption or distraction. This as a rule means a corner of an amateur work-shop—a place where there is likely to be a portable electric fire, and where soldering, brazing, grinding and other operations involving movable sources of heat, flame and sparks are carried out. It is also a place where many a man most enjoys a quiet pipe or cigarette. The hint should be sufficient, and the precautions taken should, so far as possible, be proof against any momentary forgetfulness.

Powder should be stored in the smallest convenient quantities and in the original containers. Black powder needs special care, partly to exclude moisture and partly because it is much more readily inflammable than nitro, and is the more dangerous stuff to have about. Loose powder should never be allowed to lie on the loading bench, which should be kept scrupulously clear and clean.

Caps should be treated with great respect. Powders burn: caps detonate, and if one of a tin or jar full of loose caps were accidentally set off the result could be lethal.

The powder used should always be fresh—not old, recovered or of uncertain origin, which may have suffered deterioration through improper storage. Fresh powder has a somewhat pleasant smell, derived from alcohol, ether or acetone. But powder undergoing deterioration has an irritating, acidic odour.

Equipment. The modern home-loader who requires to load and reload crimp-closed plastic cases with smokeless powders will need one of the popular loading machines, as advertised in the sporting press. Unless the machine has facilities for varying the powder and shot charges, he will also need the appropriate " bushings " or measures which fit inside it, and which determine the charges it delivers. A highly desirable, not to say indispensable, addition is an apothecary's balance for checking the powder charges at intervals, or one of the new beam balances made for the purpose.

Incidental equipment, such as containers for components, should be provided and so organised as to facilitate orderly and progressive working according to a set routine, thus enlisting the aid of habit and reducing the risk of error through absent-mindedness.

Procedure. The object here assumed is the production of safe and consistent ammunition of a certain type having well-established characteristics—not the working up of experimental loads or the pursuit of some real or imaginary advantage that has hitherto eluded the regular manufacturers. To attain this object the home-loader must stick to the book. He must recognise that *any* departure from recommended loads and components may have unpredictable results, particularly as affecting the danger-element of pressure, which he is not ordinarily equipped to measure. For example, a given charge of powder and shot may give significantly different pressures in cases, outwardly similar, but of different internal dimensions, as determined by the type of base-wad employed (see illustration opposite page 80). Pressure may also be seriously affected by what might appear to be innocent changes in the nature or dimensions of the wadding column.

So if a home-loader is using, say, Eley cases of a certain type, he must not regard himself as free to use any others that he may acquire, without having sample loads tested for pressure and velocity.

Another point: charges are properly determinable by *weight*, whereas the loading machine measures them by *volume*. But the weight of a given volume may change—for example, by the vibration of the machine, or by the amount of powder in the container. Both factors will affect the extent to which the powder packs down in the bushing. If a charge is thrown from a nearly empty container, and care is taken to avoid vibration, it may be found to be a full grain lighter than one thrown by the same bushing when the container is full, and the powder slide is moved with a jerk. Hence the need for checking the weights thrown.

The machine should thus be used in a regular manner. If the user makes a habit of tapping the slide after moving it to receive powder, he should *always* tap it, and in the same way.

Coming now to reloading, the first step, and an important one, is to examine critically the available cases.

The state of the base wad must be visually checked, and cases in which any part of it is missing should be rejected. So should any showing signs of splits, cracks or burns, or fractured or deformed heads, or heads that are not tight on the tubes. Cases should not be used if the tubes are deformed, or if the mouths are too frayed or weakened to form good, firm crimps or turn-overs.

The actual reloading operation involves eight stages—(1) de-capping; (2) re-capping; (3) charging powder; (4) seating wads; (5) charging shot; (6) starting crimp; (7) crimping, and (8) resizing.

It is especially important to check that the re-capping operation has been properly carried out and that the cap is firmly seated in the chamber, and yet flush with the cartridge head. If it protrudes, there is a danger that it may be set off by the closing of the gun. If it is loose—if it goes in without resistance—the case must be discarded. For the rest, these operations will require to be performed in accordance with the instructions issued by the manufacturers of the machine. These should be read in conjunction with the notes issued by Imperial Metal Industries (Kynoch) Ltd. for the reloading of Eley cartridges and reproduced by permission at the end of this chapter. They include all the loads likely to be required for normal use.

Requests for information on special loads should be addressed to the Sporting Ammunition Division, I.M.I. (Kynoch) Ltd., P.O. Box 216, Kynoch Works, Witton, Birmingham 6.

Black powder loads. As already indicated, black powder, though more inflammable than nitro, is more tolerant of variations in associated components and treatment, and detailed loading schedules are not required.

For 12-bore and smaller shotguns the powder should be TS2, for larger bores TS6. A police permit is required.

Paper or plastic cases may be used, primed with the ordinary 1B Eley "Surefire" cap.

Wads may be of felt or vegetable felt, such as the Eley "Kleena", loaded with an $\frac{1}{8}$-inch over-powder card. There is no critical wad pressure; the wad column should merely be firmly seated on the powder. A normally tight crimp or turnover is necessary.

As I am never asked for black powder loads below 12-bore, but often for larger gauge, I give the following selection as likely to be most useful. Except for the first two, which are general purpose loads, they are all wildfowling loads.

TABLE 7. Black Powder Loads

12-bore	$2\frac{1}{2}$ inch	(Standard)	—	3 drams powder	$1\frac{1}{8}$ oz. shot
	$2\frac{1}{2}$ inch	(Light load)	—	$2\frac{3}{4}$ "	1 "
	$2\frac{1}{2}$ inch	(Long range)	—	$2\frac{3}{4}$ "	$1\frac{1}{4}$ "
	$2\frac{3}{4}$ inch	"	—	3 "	$1\frac{1}{2}$ "
	3 inch	"	—	$3\frac{1}{4}$ "	$1\frac{3}{4}$ "
10-bore	$2\frac{5}{8}$ inch	"	—	3 "	2 "
	$2\frac{7}{8}$ inch	"	—	$3\frac{1}{4}$ "	2 "
8-bore	$3\frac{1}{4}$ inch	"	—	5 "	$2\frac{1}{2}$ "

Notes:

(1) All the above loads are suitable for sound guns of the appropriate gauge and chamber length as normally proved for black or smokeless powder.

(2) The shot size for the long-range loads should not be smaller than No. 4 for the 12-bore and No. 1 for the 8- and 10-bores.

(3) The chamber lengths shown for the 8- and 10-bores are the only ones for which Eley cases are now available.

Checking results

The home-loader would be well advised to confine himself, if possible, to one line of cartridges, whether it be for trap or skeet, or for field shooting or wildfowling. And having settled down to a steady type of production, he would be wise to send samples to the Birmingham Proof House for tests. This would reveal any undesirable characteristics and provide an invaluable guide to future operations. The cost of such tests is very reasonable, and even if the ammunition is above reproach, the reassurance is well worth the money.

The following notes by I.M.I. give all the necessary information and instructions for this purpose. (Readers using American powders and components should refer to the " Lyman Shotshell Handbook " published by the Lyman Gun Sight Corporation, Middlefield, Connecticut, which gives a large range of tested loads using this material.)

RELOADING ELEY SHOTGUN CARTRIDGES

These notes on the reloading of shotgun cartridges are offered as a guide and the Eley Ammunition Division of IMI can accept no responsibility for the performance of cartridges not loaded at their factory.

Components

(1) CASES intended for reloading should be examined carefully for soundness of head and tube and any showing signs of weakness should be discarded. Paper cases with damp tubes and waterproof cases with wet base wads must be rejected.

(2) POWDER must be kept away from heat and open flame and the container should be kept closed when not in use and stored in a cool dry place.

(3) CAPS should be selected to match the powder used. In the recommended loads tabulated overleaf it is essential that Eley Surefire caps are employed to match the Nobel-Glasgow propellant.

(4) ELEY-KLEENA WADDING is ideal for reloading. The wad diameter suits both paper and plastic fired cases and ensures perfect obturation (gas-seal) and freedom from barrel leading.

Reloading techniques

(1) CASE TRIMMING, if required, should be carried out, to the overall lengths shown in the tables.

(2) DECAPPING AND RECAPPING are simple operations and should not present any difficulty to the reloader. The decapping tool should freely enter the cap chamber without distorting or enlarging the flash hole.

TABLE 8

RECOMMENDED LOADS FOR PAPER TUBE CARTRIDGES—PRIMED WITH ELEY SUREFIRE CAPS

Gauge and chamber length (inches)	Actual case length (inches)	Type of closure	Powder		Shot charge (ounces)	Overpowder card (inches)	Main Wad Kleena (inches)	Undershot card (inches)	Overshot card (inches)
			Type (Nobel-Glasgow)	Charge (grains)					
10G $2\frac{7}{8}$	$2\frac{7}{8}$	Rolled	No. 62	38	$1\frac{7}{16}$	1/11	$\frac{3}{8}$ (2)	1/11	$\frac{1}{16}$
10G $2\frac{5}{8}$	$2\frac{5}{8}$	Rolled	No. 62	32	$1\frac{5}{16}$	1/11	$\frac{3}{8}$ (2)	1/11	$\frac{1}{16}$
12G 3	3	Crimped	No. 62	32	$1\frac{3}{8}$	$\frac{1}{8}$	$\frac{3}{8}$ (2)	—	—
12G 3	3	Rolled	No. 62	32	$1\frac{3}{8}$	1/11	$\frac{1}{2}$ (2)	—	$\frac{1}{16}$
12G $2\frac{3}{4}$	$2\frac{3}{4}$	Crimped	No. 62	32	$1\frac{1}{4}$	1/11	$\frac{1}{2}$	1/11	—
12G $2\frac{3}{4}$	$2\frac{3}{4}$	Rolled	No. 62	31	$1\frac{1}{4}$	$\frac{1}{8}$	$\frac{3}{8}$ (2)	—	$\frac{1}{16}$
12G $2\frac{1}{2}$	$2\frac{3}{4}$	Crimped	No. 62	27	$1\frac{3}{16}$	$\frac{1}{8}$	$\frac{3}{8}$ (2)	—	—
12G $2\frac{1}{2}$	$2\frac{9}{16}$	Rolled	No. 62	27	$1\frac{3}{16}$	$\frac{1}{8}$	$\frac{3}{8}$ (2)	—	$\frac{1}{16}$
12G $2\frac{1}{2}$	$2\frac{3}{4}$	Crimped	No. 62	29	$1\frac{1}{8}$	$\frac{1}{8}$	$\frac{3}{8}$ (2)	—	—
12G $2\frac{1}{2}$	$2\frac{9}{16}$	Rolled	No. 62	29	$1\frac{1}{8}$	$\frac{1}{8}$	$\frac{3}{8}$ (2)	—	$\frac{1}{16}$
*12G $2\frac{1}{2}$	$2\frac{3}{4}$	Crimped	No. 60	$24\frac{1}{2}$	$1\frac{1}{8}$	$\frac{1}{8}$	$\frac{3}{8}$ (2)	—	—
12G $2\frac{1}{2}$	$2\frac{3}{4}$	Crimped	No. 60	26	$1\frac{1}{16}$	$\frac{1}{8}$	$\frac{3}{8}$ (2)	1/11	—
12G $2\frac{1}{2}$	$2\frac{9}{16}$	Rolled	No. 60	26	$1\frac{1}{16}$	$\frac{1}{8}$	$\frac{3}{8}$ (2)	—	$\frac{1}{16}$
12G $2\frac{1}{2}$	$2\frac{9}{16}$	Crimped	No. 60	25	1	$\frac{1}{8}$	$\frac{1}{2}$	1/11	—
12G $2\frac{1}{2}$	$2\frac{9}{16}$	Crimped	No. 60	$26\frac{1}{2}$	1	$\frac{1}{8}$	$\frac{1}{2}$	1/11	—
12G $2\frac{1}{2}$	$2\frac{9}{16}$	Rolled	No. 60	$26\frac{1}{2}$	1	$\frac{1}{8}$	$\frac{3}{8}$ (2)	—	$\frac{1}{16}$
16G $2\frac{3}{4}$	$2\frac{3}{4}$	Crimped	No. 62	25	1	$\frac{1}{8}$	$\frac{1}{2}$	1/11	—
16G $2\frac{3}{4}$	$2\frac{3}{4}$	Rolled	No. 62	25	1	$\frac{1}{8}$	$\frac{3}{8}$ (2)	—	$\frac{1}{16}$
16G $2\frac{1}{2}$	$2\frac{3}{4}$	Crimped	No. 60	20	$\frac{7}{8}$	$\frac{1}{8}$	$\frac{3}{8}$ (2)	—	—
16G $2\frac{1}{2}$	$2\frac{9}{16}$	Rolled	No. 60	20	$\frac{7}{8}$	$\frac{1}{8}$	$\frac{1}{2}$	$\frac{1}{8}$	$\frac{1}{16}$
20G $2\frac{3}{4}$	$2\frac{3}{4}$	Crimped	No. 62	22	$\frac{7}{8}$	$\frac{1}{8}$	$\frac{1}{2}$	1/11	—
20G $2\frac{3}{4}$	$2\frac{3}{4}$	Rolled	No. 62	22	$\frac{7}{8}$	$\frac{1}{8}$	$\frac{3}{8}$ (2)	—	$\frac{1}{16}$
20G $2\frac{1}{2}$	$2\frac{3}{4}$	Crimped	No. 62	21	$\frac{3}{4}$	$\frac{1}{8}$	$\frac{3}{8}$ (2)	1/11	—
20G $2\frac{1}{2}$	$2\frac{9}{16}$	Rolled	No. 62	21	$\frac{3}{4}$	$\frac{1}{8}$	$\frac{3}{8}$ (2)	—	$\frac{1}{16}$

* Trapshooting load

TABLE 9

RECOMMENDED LOADS FOR PLASTIC TUBE CARTRIDGES—PRIMED WITH ELEY SURFIRE CAPS

Gauge and chamber length (inches)	Actual case length (inches)	Type of closure	Powder		Shot charge (ounces)	Overpowder card (inches)	Main Wad Kleena (inches)	Undershot card (inches)	Overshot card (inches)
			Type (Nobel-Glasgow)	Charge (grains)					
12G $2\frac{3}{4}$	$2\frac{3}{4}$	Crimped	No. 62	31	$1\frac{1}{4}$	$\frac{1}{8}$	$\frac{3}{8}$ (2)	—	—
12G $2\frac{3}{4}$	$2\frac{3}{4}$	Rolled	No. 62	31	$1\frac{1}{4}$	$\frac{1}{8}$	$\frac{3}{8}$ (2)	1/11	$\frac{1}{16}$
12G $2\frac{1}{2}$	$2\frac{3}{4}$	Crimped	No. 62	$30\frac{1}{2}$	$1\frac{3}{16}$	$\frac{1}{8}$	$\frac{3}{8}$ (2)	—	—
12G $2\frac{1}{2}$	$2\frac{9}{16}$	Rolled	No. 62	$30\frac{1}{2}$	$1\frac{3}{16}$	$\frac{1}{8}$	$\frac{3}{8}$ (2)	—	$\frac{1}{16}$
12G $2\frac{1}{2}$	$2\frac{3}{4}$	Crimped	No. 62	$29\frac{1}{2}$	$1\frac{1}{8}$	$\frac{1}{8}$	$\frac{3}{8}$ (2)	1/11	—
12G $2\frac{1}{2}$	$2\frac{9}{16}$	Rolled	No. 62	$29\frac{1}{2}$	$1\frac{1}{8}$	$\frac{1}{8}$	$\frac{3}{8}$ (2)	—	$\frac{1}{16}$
*12G $2\frac{1}{2}$	$2\frac{3}{4}$	Crimped	No. 60	$24\frac{1}{2}$	$1\frac{1}{8}$	$\frac{1}{8}$	$\frac{3}{8}$ (2)	$\frac{1}{8}$	—
12G $2\frac{1}{2}$	$2\frac{3}{4}$	Crimped	No. 60	27	$1\frac{1}{16}$	$\frac{1}{8}$	$\frac{3}{8}$ (2)	$\frac{1}{8}$	—
12G $2\frac{1}{2}$	$2\frac{9}{16}$	Rolled	No. 60	27	$1\frac{1}{16}$	$\frac{1}{8}$	$\frac{3}{8}$ (2)	—	$\frac{1}{16}$
12G $2\frac{1}{2}$	$2\frac{9}{16}$	Crimped	No. 60	$25\frac{1}{2}$	1	$\frac{1}{8}$	$\frac{3}{8}$ (2)	—	—
12G $2\frac{1}{2}$	$2\frac{9}{16}$	Rolled	No. 60	$25\frac{1}{2}$	1	$\frac{1}{8}$	$\frac{3}{8}$ (2)	1/11	$\frac{1}{16}$
16G $2\frac{3}{4}$	$2\frac{3}{4}$	Crimped	No. 62	25	1	$\frac{1}{8}$	$\frac{3}{8}$ (2)	1/11	—
16G $2\frac{3}{4}$	$2\frac{3}{4}$	Rolled	No. 62	25	1	$\frac{1}{8}$	$\frac{3}{8}$ (2)	—	$\frac{1}{16}$
16G $2\frac{1}{2}$	$2\frac{3}{4}$	Crimped	No. 60	$21\frac{1}{2}$	$\frac{7}{8}$	$\frac{1}{8}$	$\frac{3}{8}$ (2)	$\frac{1}{8}$	—
16G $2\frac{1}{2}$	$2\frac{9}{16}$	Rolled	No. 60	$21\frac{1}{2}$	$\frac{7}{8}$	$\frac{1}{8}$	$\frac{3}{8}$ (2)	—	$\frac{1}{16}$
20G $2\frac{3}{4}$	$2\frac{3}{4}$	Crimped	No. 62	21	$\frac{7}{8}$	$\frac{1}{8}$	$\frac{3}{8}$ (2)	—	—
20G $2\frac{3}{4}$	$2\frac{3}{4}$	Rolled	No. 62	21	$\frac{7}{8}$	$\frac{1}{8}$	$\frac{3}{8}$ (2)	1/11	$\frac{1}{16}$
20G $2\frac{1}{2}$	$2\frac{9}{16}$	Crimped	No. 62	$20\frac{1}{2}$	$\frac{3}{4}$	$\frac{1}{8}$	$\frac{3}{8}$ (2)	1/11	—
20G $2\frac{1}{2}$	$2\frac{9}{16}$	Rolled	No. 62	$20\frac{1}{2}$	$\frac{3}{4}$	$\frac{1}{8}$	$\frac{3}{8}$ (2)	—	$\frac{1}{16}$

* Trapshooting load

Eley cases with coppered cap chambers are made so that they may be reprimed with either Eley Surefire caps or with battery pocket primers. If the recommended loads with Nobel-Glasgow powders are being used Eley Surefire caps are essential, and it may be necessary to support the cap chamber flange when decapping these cases to ensure that the cap chamber is not removed.

(3) POWDER charges must be accurately weighed out. If the propellant is loaded by volume it is recommended that the charges are checked frequently by weight to ensure the minimum variation from the desired ballistic level. The temptation to " put an extra pinch in to give a good velocity " should be resisted.

(4) The OVERPOWDER CARD should be carefully inserted to avoid tilting but should not be rammed.

(5) WAD insertion into fired plastic cases is made easier if the case mouth is opened slightly with a tapered plug. If this is done the reloader will find the plastic cases are easier to wad than the paper cases which tend to delaminate on the inside edge at the mouth and form an obstruction to the wads.

About 50 lb. ramming should be applied to the complete wadding column when it is in the cartridge and before the shot is inserted. With the prescribed wadding column this should leave $\frac{1}{2}$ inch free length of case after the shot charge has been inserted for crimping for a paper tube and 13/32 inch free length for a plastic tube. For a rolled turnover closure 9/32 inch of the tube should remain after a $\frac{1}{16}$ inch card has been placed over the shot charge for both paper and plastic cases.

(6) CRIMPING a plastic tubed cartridge is simplified if a " crimp starter " is used to press the plastic folds into position before the conventional coned re-crimping die is used.

Re-crimping paper case cartridges and re-closing paper and plastic cases with a rolled turnover should present no difficulties.

Care should be taken to avoid loose shot or free space in the cartridge and any looseness should be taken up by adjusting the length of the wadding column.

(7) RESIZING cartridges after loading is recommended especially for plastic cartridges to reduce the excessive step between the tube and the head. This operation will also smooth out any shot bulges which may have occurred when the crimp was consolidated.

Performance

For consistent cartridge performance and also for the higher velocity levels a factory loaded product is essential. Nevertheless, with care and attention the reloader can achieve adequate results with medium power cartridges using the recommended loads.

If, however, it is suspected that the reloaded cartridges are showing a tendency towards weak shooting and this is confirmed by the presence of unburnt powder in the barrel, the performance can often be improved by increasing the strength of the closure. This may be achieved by varnishing the crimp in a paper case, or by increasing the ramming on the wadding column and deepening the crimp closure on a plastic case. Similar techniques may also assist in maintaining the ballistic levels of paper and plastic cartridges with rolled turnover closures.

Laboratory reports on hand loads

The Birmingham Proof House is equipped and willing to test and report on hand loaded shotgun cartridges from any source. Reports normally cover pressure at 1 in. and 6 in. from the breech, velocity over 40 yards and recoil. Reports can be given (but are not normally given) on shot patterns at 40 yards. One cartridge of each loading is broken down and report issued as to the load, components and turnover resistance or pull. (A loading check is essential to safeguard valuable laboratory equipment.) Submitters are asked to advise the loads used quoting type and weight of powder and weight of shot.

The cost of such reports at present is £2 2. 0. for up to eleven cartridges of one gauge and chamber length, and 1s. 6d. each for extra cartridges of the same gauge and chamber length. It is recommended that not less than six and preferably eleven cartridges of each loading be submitted for test. Reports will normally be issued within four days of receipt of cartridges.

Cartridges must not be sent through the post. They may be sent by passenger train or road carrier clearly labelled " Ammunition Class 6 Division 1—Safety Cartridges—Not Liable to Explode in Bulk ".

Cartridges should be addressed to the Laboratory, The Birmingham Proof House, Banbury Street, Birmingham, 5.

Owing to the vagaries of home-loading, all information in this chapter is given without responsibility.

Plastic wads. The loads set out in Tables 8 and 9 may be used with plastic-skirted wads such as the Eley Monowad or the new British Plaswad. Pending specific pressure tests, however, powder charges associated with such wads should be reduced by 10 per cent.

CHAPTER NINE

WEIGHT AND RECOIL

THE BASIC principle involved in the recoil of guns was laid down by Sir Isaac Newton three centuries ago. According to his Third Law of Motion, the momentum of the recoiling gun is always equal to the momentum of the issuing charge. And since momentum is *Weight* × *Velocity*, the principle may be expressed as follows—

The weight multiplied by the velocity of the recoiling gun equals the weight multiplied by the velocity of the issuing charge.

From this it follows that—

$$\text{Velocity of recoil} = \frac{\text{Wt. of charge}}{\text{Wt. of gun}} \times \text{velocity of charge}$$

(*Note*: In working out practical examples all weights must be in the same units; and the weight of the charge must include the weight of the wads and, say, 50 per cent of the weight of the powder.)

In a work as comprehensive and recent as Burrard's *The Modern Shotgun*, this is the only aspect of recoil considered, it being laid down that the acceptable limit of recoil in a sporting gun is a velocity of about 16 feet per second.

But the recoil of a firearm supported by a shooter and braced against his shoulder cannot be disposed of so simply: it is necessary to consider what I will call (1) the dynamic recoil, and (2) the sensible recoil.

(1) The dynamic recoil is the recoil determined by Newton's law already explained. The weight and velocity of the shot charge being settled, the gun's recoil is decided by its weight,

provided it has a solid breech and no muzzle-brake, in which case, to keep the velocity of recoil down to Burrard's 16 feet per second it is usually necessary that the gun should weigh about 96 times the shot charge, or 6 lb. of gun to every ounce of shot.

But if the gun has a moving breech, like those of the recoil-operated automatics, an appreciable portion of the energy of the recoil is absorbed by friction in the barrel-braking system, the actual amount being variable and dependent on lubrication, as many users of long-recoil automatics who have been too free with the oil-can have found to their cost.

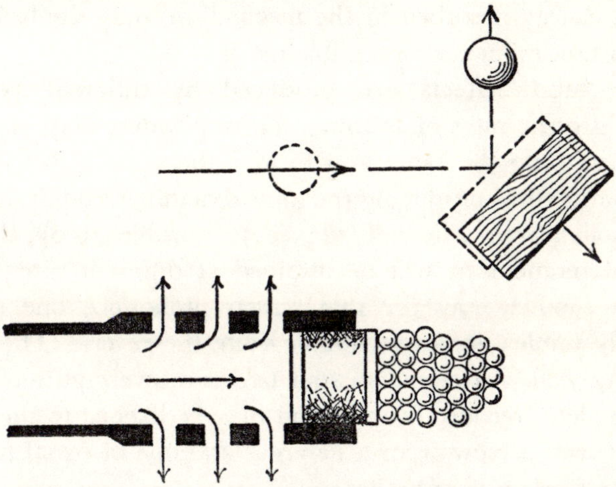

Fig. 22. Principle of muzzle-brake. Ball deflected from wooden block on floor exerts reaction on block causing it to move as shown. Sideways deflection of barrel gases through slots of muzzle-brake exerts similar reaction on slots' forward edges, thus reducing recoil.

Dynamic recoil in single-barrelled guns is also affected by whether or not a muzzle-brake is fitted. These brakes work by permitting a substantial part of the high velocity gas following the shot charge up the barrel to escape sideways through slots formed near the muzzle. The diversion of this gas sideways sets up strong reactive forces on the forward edges of the slots, thus tending to throw the barrel forward, and partly counteracting the pressure on the breech which initiates the recoil. (See fig. 22.)

These brakes, incidentally, can introduce unpleasant blast effects.

(2) The sensible recoil, or recoil as felt by the shooter, can be defined as the net effect of the dynamic recoil on his physical and nervous organisation. This is the aspect of recoil which really matters. For a given dynamic recoil the sensible recoil can vary considerably. For example, a shooter firing an ill-fitting gun, which kicks his face and bruises his arm, might find the recoil from a given charge intolerable, but not so if the gun were made to fit him snugly by a mere alteration of the stock or the addition of a recoil pad. The particular system of springs used for absorbing and utilising the recoil of self-loading weapons, and the energy absorbed in the mechanism, may similarly have an important influence on sensible recoil.

More subtle effects are produced by different powders, giving different rates of burning. These powders may be loaded successively into the same gun to give the same velocity to the same charge, thus producing the same dynamic recoil, in terms of final momentum. But not the same sensible recoil, because the final momentum will be attained at different rates, and a sensitive shooter may for this reason pronounce one powder decidedly unpleasant and another quite the reverse. The difference may well correspond to that between severe gun-headache and complete freedom from it, and may be likened to the difference between a blow from a hammer and one of equal momentum from a soft rubber mallet.

An old fallacy

It is widely believed that the slow-growing momentum of recoil imparted to a gun by a progressive or slow-burning powder produces less sensible recoil than a quick-burning powder, other things being equal. This belief has been completely undermined by rigorous and prolonged scientific experiments, and must, it seems, now be discarded as a popular fallacy. It has been much fostered by the fact that earlier " sweet-burning " powders, such as the old Amberite, gave somewhat low ballistics.

The more modern approach to the reduction of sensible recoil was first brought to my notice by a famous Birmingham gunmaker. He was developing a special-purpose gun, the recoil of which was excessive, yet he was barred from reducing the weight or velocity of the projectile or increasing the weight of the gun. He found his solution in the use of an ultra-quick-burning propellant. It might be thought that this would give an abnormally painful hammer blow, but in fact the blow was too quick for the shooter's nervous system to appreciate.

It is a matter of common experience that sensation does not follow instantly on stimulus: there is an appreciable time-lag, which is why we intuitively snatch a splinter out of a wound instead of drawing it out gently. We know that if only we can be quick enough, the splinter will be gone before the pain has time to develop. Indeed, if the stimulus, however violent it may be, is only sufficiently transitory, it may fail completely to awaken pain. "I never felt anything of it at the time," is the common experience of those who suffer grave and painful injuries from very sudden happenings.

This, then, is the explanation of how the Birmingham gunmaker arrived at his solution. Nevertheless, it is a hard principle to demonstrate. It cannot be demonstrated by firing one or two cartridges, differently loaded, in cold blood, for even the frame of mind in which a gun is fired can have a big influence on sensible recoil. Who has not noticed the curiously heavy recoil when a familiar gun loaded with a familiar cartridge is fired deliberately at a mark? Yet the recoil of the same gun and cartridge fired in the course of sport may seem light and pleasant. To demonstrate the influence of rate of burning on sensible recoil requires a prolonged course of scientifically controlled experiments, such as those carried out by I.M.I. when they were developing their modern range of powders and ammunition. These were the experiments I have already mentioned. They involved the firing of many thousands of cartridges by a team of nine experienced shots of varying build, shooting under a wide variety of conditions with guns of different types, weight and boring. The cartridges were all loaded to give the same velocity to the same shot charge, though by means of powders of various rates of burning. The shooters did not know what they were firing, but were merely required to give marks for recoil. They were unanimous in assigning the lowest recoil to the cartridges loaded with the fastest-burning powder, the dynamical effect of which was checked throughout by electric accelerometers built into the stocks of the guns, and their conclusions have since been widely confirmed.

To summarise, therefore, the dynamic recoil, hitherto regarded as the sole measure of recoil in practical shooting, is now seen merely as its broad determinant. In fixed-breech guns, and in the absence of a muzzle-brake, it is settled by their weight in relation to the weight and velocity of the charge. In moving-breech guns it may be modified, as, for example, by the frictional-braking of the recoiling barrel. The effect of the dynamic recoil on the shooter, or the sensible recoil, which, as I have said, is the recoil that really matters, is in turn modified by a number of factors, chief among which are gun-fit and the rate of burning of the powder. It follows that the recoil-sensitive individual and particularly the gun-headache sufferer may find relief in one or other of several ways—not merely or necessarily in a lighter charge or a heavier gun, or in a better-fitted stock or a recoil pad, but possibly in a faster-burning powder, or even, if the conditions of his sport admit of his using such a weapon, in a repeater, such as the F. N. Browning 2-shot, or a pump-gun fitted with a muzzle-brake.

Pathological cases

There remain the cases of guns, apparently normal in every respect, which recoil painfully with standard ammunition. This may arise from some vagary of boring such as an enlargement immediately in front of the chamber cone, caused, for example, by allowing a polishing lap to dwell unduly at the end of its travel.

Perhaps a more familiar cause is an undue clearance (i.e. headspace clearance) between the cartridge head and the standing breech. In *Gough Thomas's Gun Book* I have given examples and details of effective cures, including the soldering of thin circular " shims " to the breech face.

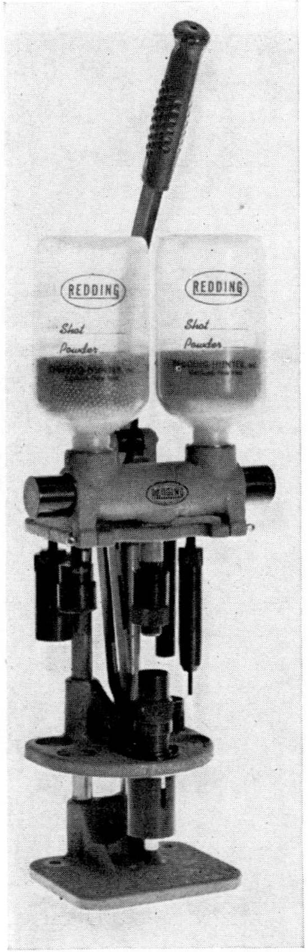

Left : A popular loading machine, the Redding Model 16

Above right : A beam balance, an indispensable accessory for the home-loader. This Redding model has a maximum capacity of 325 grains and is guaranteed accurate to within 0.1 grain

Below right : The Westley Richards single trigger. This ingenious device, applied to both shotguns and big game double rifles, is one of the most celebrated and successful of all selective single trigger mechanisms

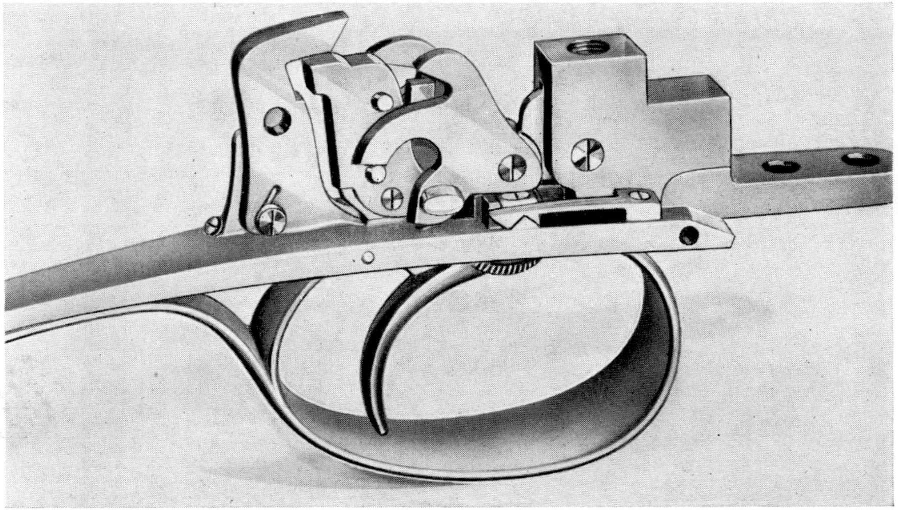

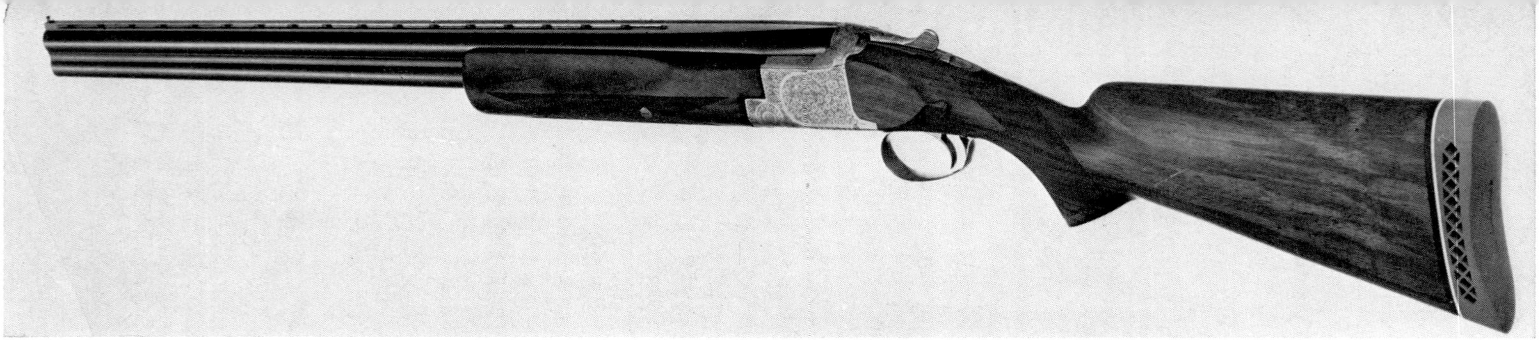

An F.N. Browning over-and-under trap gun. This celebrated model is perhaps the most widely favoured of all double-barrelled guns for clay pigeon shooting

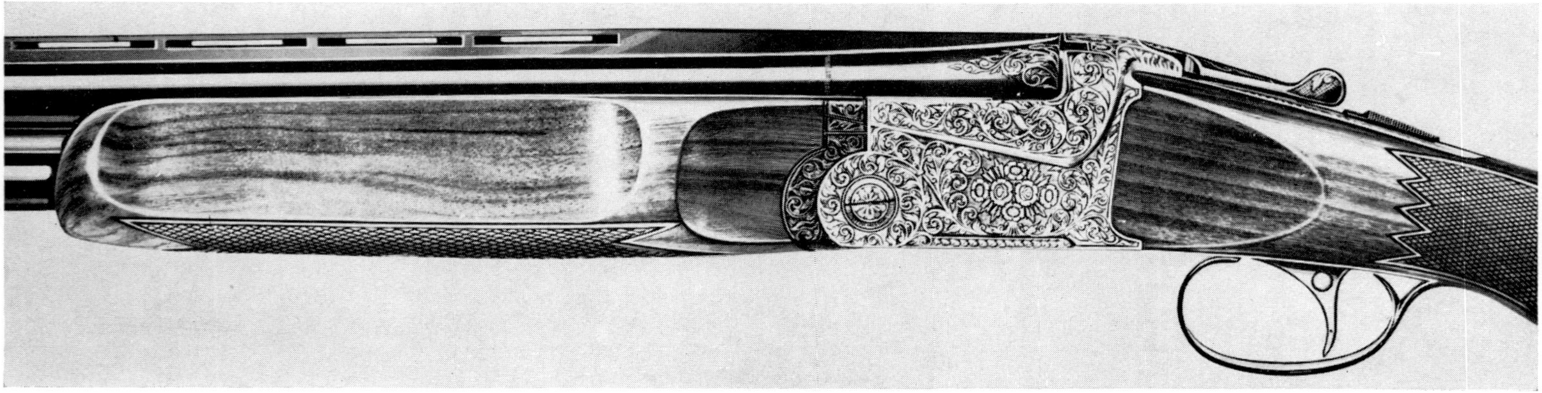

An S.K.B. over-and-under trap gun. This B.S.A.-sponsored Japanese weapon is a strong challenger to European models

CHAPTER TEN

CLAY PIGEON GUNS

THE INCREASING popularity of clay pigeon shooting requires special consideration of the guns used for the three main divisions of this sport, namely—

1. Trap or Down-the-Line (D.T.L.), including Olympic Trench
2. Skeet
3. Sporting

All guns used for these competitive sports have certain requirements in common. Thus, they must be efficient from every point of view, because a single bird lost may lose a major competition. They must accordingly throw the best quality, the most suitable and the most consistent patterns of which the available ammunition is capable, and must deliver them to the right place. The guns should be well fitted and well balanced, and should point easily and naturally, and should not harbour any feature of form or function likely to irritate the shooter or distract his attention, whether consciously or subconsciously. Several of these points are elaborated later, or in other chapters.

Type of gun. For informal or non-competitive shooting, any ordinary 12-bore game gun can be used. For trap, at least one well-choked barrel is desirable, and for skeet, the reverse. For sporting clays, the ordinary game gun has a claim to be regarded as the proper weapon.

For serious competitive work, the British shooter appears to have decided overwhelmingly in favour of the over-and-under (O/U). The reason for this is not entirely clear, since Continental live-pigeon trap-shooters, engaged in a similar but even more exacting sport, favour the side-by-side. But I have examined this question elsewhere* and will not pursue it now.

The reasons usually given for the popularity of the O/U are that it prints its second or top barrel pattern somewhat higher than it does the first or bottom one, which is advantageous for second shots at rising birds. In addition, it is considered to be more "pointable". American shooters seem to prefer the pump or slide-action, perhaps because it provokes a vigorous recovery of direction after the first shot. This, like the high-shooting second barrel of the O/U, may compensate for a natural tendency to shoot low with the second shot. But the O/U and the self-loaders are also favoured in the U.S., though I have an impression that the latter are declining in favour here.

The normal gun for trap and skeet in this country is thus a 12-bore over-and-under with $2\frac{1}{2}$- or $2\frac{3}{4}$-inch chambers, adapted for firing the standard $1\frac{1}{8}$ oz. load.

(For Olympic trench, the $1\frac{1}{4}$ oz. load is used, for which the gun must have $2\frac{3}{4}$-inch chambers.)

The trap gun usually has 30-inch choked barrels. For protection against recoil, it is of full weight—$7\frac{1}{2}$ to $8\frac{1}{4}$ lb. Since the gun is shouldered before calling for the bird, the stock is longer and straighter than that of a game gun, with a high, level comb for accurate positioning of the shooter's aiming eye.

The rib is raised, knurled and ventilated, often with a mid-sight in addition to the normal foresight. The triggers may be double or single. If the latter, the gun usually has a pistol grip or half-pistol.

The gun for skeet is similar to the trap gun except that it has shorter open-bored barrels, usually 26 inches in length. It is often the same gun, fitted with an alternative pair of barrels.

Borings. The trap gun is usually bored half to full choke in the bottom barrel and full in the top one.

The skeet gun is usually bored true cylinder and improved cylinder, or improved cylinder in both barrels.

Continental guns now bear "star markings" indicative of the degree of choke in their barrels at the time of proof. These markings are as follows:

* See *Gough Thomas's Gun Book*—A. & C. Black, Ltd., London

*= 0.9—1.0 mm.	(full choke)
**= 0.7—0.8 mm.	(three-quarter choke)
***= 0.4—0.5—0.6 mm.	(half choke)
****= 0.2—0.3 mm.	(improved cylinder)
CL =	(true cylinder)

It should be particularly noted, however, that *these markings are dimensional indications only*, and convey little or no assurance that the patterns thrown by a given cartrige will be of corresponding density. Now that there are several inexpensive clay pigeon guns on the market it is important that their performance should not be taken on trust. Some Continental guns, for example, are over-choked, and actually give closer patterns when some of the choke is removed.

Some shooters take it for granted that the best boring for a trap gun is full and full; but they may find, especially if they are naturally quick, but in one of the lower handicap groups, that they can do better with a more open-bored first barrel, and with No. 8 shot rather than No. 7.

Single-barrelled trap and skeet guns can, of course, be fitted with replaceable choke tubes or collet-type variable chokes, though not with muzzle-brakes under C.P.S.A. rules; but the performance of these devices, particularly the latter, should be checked. (See page 67 " Variable chokes".)

Mean point of impact. The serious trap or skeet shooter must infallibly check his patterns and their mean point of impact (MPI) in relation to the point of aim. The normal O/U prints its top barrel pattern, say, 6 to 9 inches above that of the bottom barrel. But this distance varies from gun to gun, perhaps to an extent sufficient to prejudice performance. It may be unduly exaggerated, or it may be reduced to nothing. It may even go into reverse—that is to say, the barrels may cross-shoot in the vertical plane. The only feasible remedy for any abnormality here is eccentric choking, not normally practised by the English gun trade.

Over-and-under guns also need checking for lateral deviation of the MPI, particularly if they are cast-off. Cases have come to my notice in which the deviation is sufficient to affect results. The cure is to remove the cast-off and to restore fit by a slight reduction of the comb height, which enables the shooter's head to lean over sufficiently to restore the alignment of rib and eye.

Holding the pattern. Some expert clay shooters value their guns according to whether or not they " hold the pattern ". The implication is that, in the course of a round of shooting, the density or quality of the patterns may deteriorate.

What actually happens, or may happen, is that when one barrel only of a double gun is repeatedly fired, whereby it becomes much warmer than the other, unequal thermal expansion causes the whole barrel assembly to warp, whereby the MPI may shift sufficiently to affect results. The direction of shift will be away from the hot barrel.

Even with sustained accuracy of pointing by the shooter, the target may thus no longer be caught by the dense central part of the pattern, but by the thinner outer zone, thus giving the impression of a deterioration of pattern quality.

According to my calculations, an effective temperature difference of 50 degrees F. between the two barrels of a 12-bore O/U gun would cause the axis of the barrel assembly to warp until it conformed to an arc of a circle of about 250 feet radius, and that the MPI would thus shift by some 12 inches at 35 yards. Practical tests support this conclusion and endorse the practice of many trap-shooters of always firing both barrels, irrespective of whether or not they have scored with the first.

It appears that this waste of ammunition could be avoided if the barrels of trap guns were made on the ribless plan, being rigidly assembled at the breech only, and joined at the muzzle by a sliding dovetail or the like, whereby each barrel would be free to expand independently of the other.

Even a single-barrelled gun may be affected in this way if the barrel has any inequality of mass around its circumference, such as might result from variation in wall-thickness or from its having a heavy rib. After a few quick shots, and until it was thermally stabilised, such a barrel would warp and shoot more or less inaccurately according to circumstances.

Triggers and trigger pulls. The triggers of the clay pigeon gun may be double or single. Here the strong arguments in favour of the double trigger (see Chapter 2) either largely do not apply or are invalidated by the single trigger's capacity to promote greater accuracy with the second shot.

The weight of the trigger pulls is a matter for individual preference, though a light pull, if the shooter is happy with it, is advantageous. The quality of the pulls should be above reproach—clean, crisp and totally free from drag.

In this country, triggers are invariably of the normal "pull" variety, though the merits of the release trigger*, briefly referred to on page 24, are believed to be gaining recognition abroad. The release trigger has the effect of cutting out the sudden access of nervous and muscular tension immediately preceding the shooter's decision to fire, and the alternative name by which it is known—the relaxation trigger—may well have some special significance for the competitive shooter.

In a two-triggered trap or skeet gun, various combinations of normal and release triggers are possible. For example, Perazzi offer release/release or release/pull—the latter a fascinating arrangement, as can be realised even by going through the necessary motions without a gun.

Testing and appraisal of patterns. I have previously stressed the importance of checking patterns. There is no room in the mind of a competitive shooter for any doubt or distrust of his gun's performance. But valid conclusions on patterns cannot be drawn from tests carelessly or ignorantly performed. In *Gough Thomas's Gun Book* I have gone fully into the testing of guns for pattern and can now only emphasise the need for tests to be *properly* performed and *correctly* interpreted.

A shooter could almost certainly score higher with an imperfect gun in which he has blind confidence than he could with a somewhat better one which he distrusts on a false appraisal.

* See "The Release Trigger" by Gough Thomas—*Shooting Times & Country Magazine*, November, 1969

CHAPTER ELEVEN

MAGNUM GUNS

THE TERM " magnum " is nowadays loosely applied to any shotgun normally firing a heavier load than that previously associated with the calibre concerned.

There is, of course, nothing new about the magnum principle. In the muzzle-loading days the shooter was free to increase his load according to circumstances, and up to the limit of his ability to stand recoil. But although he did not hesitate to take advantage of this flexibility to meet the needs of special occasions, he learned to prefer for general shooting the more moderate charges from which our own notions of standard loads were in due course derived.

The breechloader with its fixed ammunition naturally substituted certain rigidities for this flexibility, and to meet the special needs for which the muzzle-loader provided so easily we have long had variants of the common $2\frac{1}{2}$-inch cartridges, such as those with $2\frac{3}{4}$- and 3-inch cases, each carrying its appropriately increased load. But, as I explained in Chapter 7, with the development of progressive powders this process has gone much further, especially in America. There, all bores have been promoted one or even two stages in recent decades. Their standard case in the medium bores used to be $2\frac{5}{8}$ inches: it is now $2\frac{3}{4}$. The standard load for a 12-bore used to be $1\frac{1}{8}$ oz. of shot. Later, the same charge was loaded into 16-bore cases, and, later still into 20-bore, and so on through the range. As much as $1\frac{7}{8}$ oz. is being crammed into the 3-inch, 12-bore case.

These magnum guns have attracted many devotees. When compared with the larger bores firing the same charges, they possess the advantages of superior lightness, elegance and fast-handling quality, and there can be no doubt that the very word magnum has a powerful psychological appeal.

A clear challenge. As made by a leading English gunmaker, the 20- and 16-bores, firing 1 oz. and 1⅛ oz. of shot respectively, but weighing anything up to half a pound less than the corresponding 2½-inch 12-bore, are sufficiently attractive to present the latter with a clear challenge, and to provoke the question as to whether it should continue to be regarded as the proper gun for firing standard British charges, or whether it is not out of date.

The case against the small-bore magnums, which I myself have more than once argued in the *Shooting Times*, is based on two considerations: first, that, charge for charge and velocity for velocity, they must weigh the same as the corresponding 12-bore if they are not to exceed its recoil; and secondly, that their longer shot-columns expose more pellets to abrasion and deformation in their course up the barrel, which is bound to impair patterns and diminish their efficiency by increasing "stringing", or the elongation of the shot charge in flight.

Nevertheless, because of the popularity attained by these highly-charged little guns in the U.S.A. and the foothold they have gained in Europe, particularly in France, I felt a little while ago that the time was ripe to review the whole issue. I accordingly addressed enquiries on the subject to our leading gunmakers and ammunition experts and to eminent authorities in France, Belgium and Spain, with several of whom I had subsequent discussions. Easily the best case for the challengers is that put forward in a pamphlet published by the French gunmaker and magnum specialist, M. Kerné, who attributes a lower sensible recoil to the magnums by virtue of the progressive powder they employ.

But after carefully considering all the evidence placed at my disposal, including the results of the recoil experiments described in Chapter 9, and taking special note of certain features in the evidence of Kerné, I came to the conclusion that *the verdict must go to the 2½- or 2¾-inch 12-bore as being still the supremely effective weapon, in the hands of the average shooter, for firing the standard game charges favoured in this country.* I am satisfied that the small-bore magnums do not, in general, throw such good patterns, and that their lighter weight has to be purchased by some loss of velocity or increase in recoil, or both.

How then is the success of the magnum to be accounted for? I believe there are several reasons, namely—

(a) The more walking and less shooting a man does in the course of a day's sport the more he will be willing to buy lightness at the expense of recoil. The average American, we are told, fires only about 50 cartridges a year. We are also told that the average *chasseur* in France spends much of his time "marching and countermarching" and greatly values a light and well balanced gun. Under these conditions, the small-bore magnum might well be justified.

(b) In the hands of a one-gun man pursuing different kinds of sport, a small-bore magnum can provide the flexibility of the old muzzle-loader—a light charge for dogging or walking-up birds shootable at easy range, and a heavy charge for an occasional shot at wildfowl.

(c) The large-bore magnum, the 12, enables the shooter to fire the heavy charges needed for duck and goose shooting in certain circumstances without resorting to a larger bore, which may not be available, or legally permitted or within his purse.

(d) An American sceptic, whose views I quote without comment, attributes even greater importance than I have suggested to the psychological appeal of the magnum. To his countrymen, he says, it is a virility symbol.

But a pointed question remains: has the small-bore magnum achieved an *enduring* success? I am told by a reliable informant that there are distinct signs in America of a return to the lightly loaded 12-bore for game shooting. Time will tell.

CHAPTER TWELVE

BALANCE

I MUST now pick up a point involved in the choice of a gun which I could not deal with adequately in Chapter 3. It is so important in my view as to deserve a chapter to itself.

In these days, when the highest quality conventional guns are out of the reach of the average sportsman—out of the reach indeed, of most men whose fathers and grandfathers went to Purdey, Boss or Holland for their guns as a matter of course—there is some likelihood that a generation may grow up to whom fine balance in a sporting gun is a source of pleasure of which they have had no adequate experience. That would be a pity, for as I have previously said, it is hard to overrate the value of balance, or the pleasure and economy of effort with which it enables a gun to be used in the field.

So far as the mere transporting of a gun is concerned, weight, of course, is practically all that matters. It is when a gun comes into action—when it is raised and swung here and there on to swiftly-moving marks—that the virtue of good balance really stands out.

What then is balance, meaning good balance? There are many who believe that the balance of a gun is determined by the point at which it balances, see-saw fashion, when poised on the edge of the forefinger. Others believe that it is a mysterious and altogether indefinable quality that somehow attaches itself to the costly productions of famous gunmaking firms. But the subject can neither be comprehended nor dismissed so simply.

A dynamic quality

Properly regarded, balance is bound up with movement and

energy. A clue to its real nature is to be found in an expression for which I believe we are indebted to the Americans—" a fast-handling gun ". Such a gun is one that, with a minimum expenditure of energy on the part of the user, can be swung quickly and easily from one position to another, and more

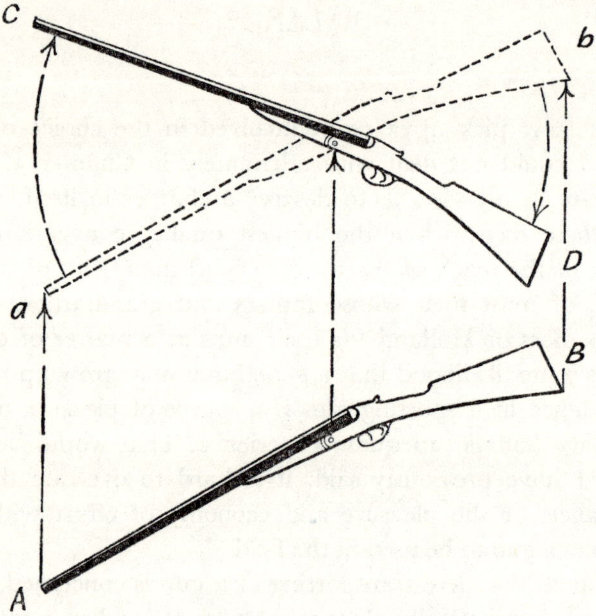

Fig. 23. Composite gun movement resolved into components. Movement of gun from, say, carrying position A-B to firing position C-D is same as if movement were executed in two stages, i.e. from A-B to a-b, without change of direction, and thence to C-D by rotation about point of balance. Energy required for executing first stage is proportional to weight only of gun; that required for second stage is proportional to gun's moment of inertia.

particularly from the carrying position to the shoulder. Now, for the purposes of analysis, this single movement can be regarded as a combination of two movements—one being a change of position without change of direction, and the other merely a change of direction (see fig. 23); and the science of dynamics teaches us that the amount of energy we have to put into the first of these movements—the change of position—is proportional simply to the weight of the gun, while that absorbed by the second—the change of direction—is proportional to the way in which the weight is distributed fore and aft. Whether the weight is dispersed towards the ends or concentrated towards the middle makes no difference to the amount of energy required to change the position, but it makes a world of difference to that required to change the direction.

Balance, therefore, is not determinable by any static test, but rather by the amount of energy demanded from the shooter in the active use of the gun, and by the way in which the effort is distributed between the hands. By reference to simple dynamical principles, it may be shown that this energy is in turn largely determined by what is called the gun's *moment of inertia* as measured about the point of balance—an engineer's expression, which takes into account not only the weight but also the way in which it is distributed. If, with two guns of the same weight, and balancing at the same point, one has its weight more concentrated between the hands, it will have a lower moment of inertia than the other. For that reason, it will be better-balanced and faster-handling, and will make less demand on the energies of its user in the process of active shooting. It will also be proportionately more pleasant to use. Viewed this way, balance and its index—the moment of inertia—may be seen to represent, possibly, the difference between hard work and pleasant exercise, between fatigue and buoyancy; and between missing and clean kills at the end of the day.

There is a further point. The moment of inertia of a gun varies according to the point or axis about which it is measured. It is least if measured about the point of balance, and it is important that this point should fall naturally about half-way between the hands. The reason for this is that when one attempts to change the direction of a gun by a relative movement of the hands, it tends to turn about the point of the least moment of inertia; and it is clearly desirable that the point about which the gun *tends* to turn should be the same as that about which one is trying to *make* it turn. If these two points are materially separated, the gun will feel unresponsive or even at odds with its user, and a gun that is conspicuously muzzle-heavy (or, for that matter, butt-heavy, like some automatics with inertia-weights in the stock) can give this feeling strongly and unpleasantly.

Good balance defined

Summing up, therefore, good balance and fast handling are attained by a gun which is as light as it can be, having due regard for recoil; which has the lowest possible value for its least moment of inertia; and which realises this value at a point about mid-way between the hands.

But this is not quite all, for the muscular sensations to which these purely mechanical properties give rise combine in the brain of the user with tactile sensations derived from the shape, smoothness and fitness to the hand of the parts of the gun actually handled. So, to complete the total effect of a finely balanced gun, it is necessary to specify that the external shape shall be elegant, with fluent lines and well finished surfaces, conformable to the hand and pleasant to the sense of touch.

With guns in which the natural disposition of weight is either forwards, or unduly dispersed, such as in the various repeaters, all this is difficult if not impossible of attainment, even with the help of glass fibres and aluminium alloys. With guns in which the disposition of weight is more central, such as box-lock doubles, the prescription can be filled with due care in design and construction. With sidelocks, it is easier, though more costly. It is perhaps easiest of all with guns of the Darne type, because of the naturally rearward disposition of weight. There is no excuse for even a cheap gun of this kind not being well balanced.

The prescription I have given for a well balanced gun merely puts into semi-technical language what generations of gun-makers have found out empirically. Over the years, they have lightened their guns by taking advantage of smokeless powders to reduce barrel lengths and to lighten them forward; they have hollowed-out stocks, and in some cases they have cleverly brought the mass of metal around the breech closer into the right hand. By so doing, they have not only got rid of weight, but have much reduced the moment of inertia and thereby improved balance and fast-handling quality.

Measuring balance

It is instructive to leave generalities and to get down to some figures. There is no difficulty in measuring the moment of inertia of a gun. I use for this purpose a kind of torsion balance—a simple device consisting of a gun-cradle fitted with a spirit level and suspended from a ceiling by a high-tensile steel wire, which is carefully fixed at both ends in rigid attachments (see fig. 24). The gun being secured in the cradle and adjusted by the help of the spirit level so that its point of balance coincides with the axis of the wire, it is made to oscillate gently and freely in a horizontal plane, whereupon the time taken to perform a given number of oscillations is taken with a stop watch. Having calibrated the wire and the empty cradle beforehand, the moment of inertia of the gun can be readily calculated. Further, if we know its value for a particular gun, we can work out where

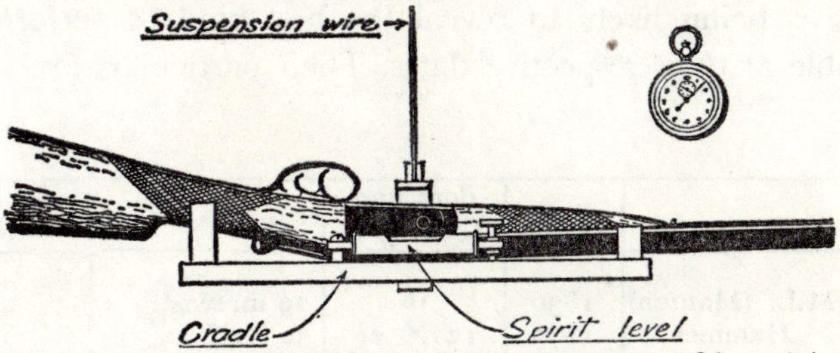

Fig. 24. Apparatus for measuring balance (moment of inertia) of gun.

the weight is effectively concentrated, and can thus assess the skill that has gone into the designing and building of it in this most important respect. I think it will be clear that if the total weight of the gun were divided equally in two, there would be two points, equidistant from the point of balance, where the half-weights could be effectively concentrated without altering the "feel" or balance in any way. The black spots in fig. 25

represent the half-weights concentrated in this manner; and in view of the gunmaker's constant endeavour to centralise the weight, it will be realised that a large value for the distance "D" is bad, and implies a gun that is lumpish and inert, while a short distance is meritorious and indicates a lively one. The

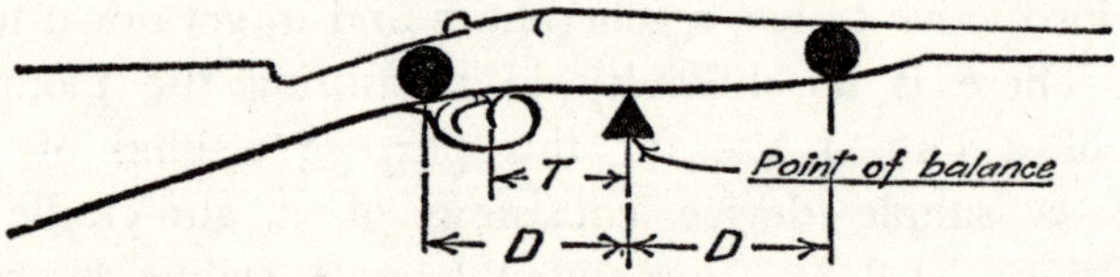

Fig. 25. Equivalent distribution of weight. Black spots represent positions where half-weights of gun could theoretically be concentrated without altering "feel" or balance.

distance "T" should preferably not exceed about $4\frac{1}{4}$ inches. If it is much more than that the gun will begin to feel heavy forward and, for reasons previously explained, at odds with its user.

As a first exercise, I chose an historical sequence of four top-quality, London-made, double-barrelled guns by celebrated makers as being likely to reveal the best kind of performance attainable at their respective dates. Their particulars are set out below.

Gun No.	*Type*	*Date*	*Bore and Chambers*	*Barrels*	*Weight (lb.)*
1	M.L. (Manton)	1830	16	29 in. twist	$6\frac{1}{4}$
2	Hammer	1875	12 × $2\frac{1}{2}$	30 in. damascus	$6\frac{3}{4}$
3	H.E.	1900	,,	30 in. steel	$6\frac{3}{4}$
4	H.E.	1948	,,	27 in. steel	6 lb. 3 oz.

In like order, these guns gave the results set out in Table 10. (The units, by the way, in which the moments of inertia are measured are what is known as gravitational or "g" units; but that need not concern us here because we are only considering the results comparatively.)

This is a notable record of improvement. It will be seen that

TABLE 10. Balance Data—Best Guns

Gun No.	*Actual Moment of Inertia in g units*	*Moment of Inertia as per cent of No. 1*	*D (ins.)*	*T (ins.)*
1	0.181	100	11.5	6
2	0.151	83	10.3	5
3	0.136	75	9.7	$4\frac{1}{2}$
4	0.099	55	8.6	$4\frac{1}{4}$

over the period in question, weight has been centralised and brought back, while the moment of inertia has been reduced by no less than 45 per cent. The energy required to manipulate the modern gun in active shooting should thereby be reduced in much the same proportion. Practical handling entirely confirms this conclusion and the high importance I have attached to balance in this chapter. It is indeed hard work handling the old Manton; but the modern 12 seems to leap into action almost by itself. The last mentioned gun, in fact, is probably the best-balanced 12-bore in its class I have ever handled. The intermediate guns have just the intermediate qualities the figures would suggest.

By way of comparison, I measured corresponding values for the following $2\frac{3}{4}$-inch, 12-bore Continental guns, namely (5) a low-priced model Darne, (6) an Italian long-recoil automatic, (7) a popular Belgian box-lock, and (8) a well-known Italian over-and-under. These guns gave the results set out below.

TABLE 11. Balance Data—Other Guns

Gun No.	*Actual Moment of Inertia in g units*	*Moment of Inertia as per cent of No. 1*	*D (ins.)*	*T (ins.)*
5	0.126	70	9.7	$3\frac{1}{4}$
6	0.136	75	9.5	$5\frac{1}{2}$
7	0.141	78	10.0	$4\frac{7}{8}$
8	0.151	83	10.0	5

As might have been foreseen, the Darne came best out of this selection, though its moment of inertia was higher than expected. The secret of its handling quality evidently lay largely in its forward lightness, as indicated by its abnormally low value of $3\frac{1}{4}$ inches for *T*.

The rest of the guns were without this redeeming feature; but as they all had $2\frac{3}{4}$-inch chambers, they were not strictly comparable with the English guns from a technical point of view. They were nevertheless representative of guns commonly being bought here today to fire the same standard $2\frac{1}{2}$-inch cartridge, and may thus be taken, not unfairly, to illustrate my original point, by showing how far certain popular guns fall short of the standards of balance, liveliness and fast-handling that have been attained by the best guns hitherto made in this country.

There is one concluding point on balance generally, and that is that the best balanced guns go beyond what some regard as the optimum in fast-handling quality: they prefer a slower gun as being steadier and less likely to encourage checking the swing. This, of course, is a legitimate personal preference and one that might be entertained in relation to a particular kind of shooting only. The fastest-handling guns show at their best at such sport as partridge driving or rabbit, pigeon or woodcock shooting in covert, and the slowest-handling types are least disadvantageous in duck flighting or the like.

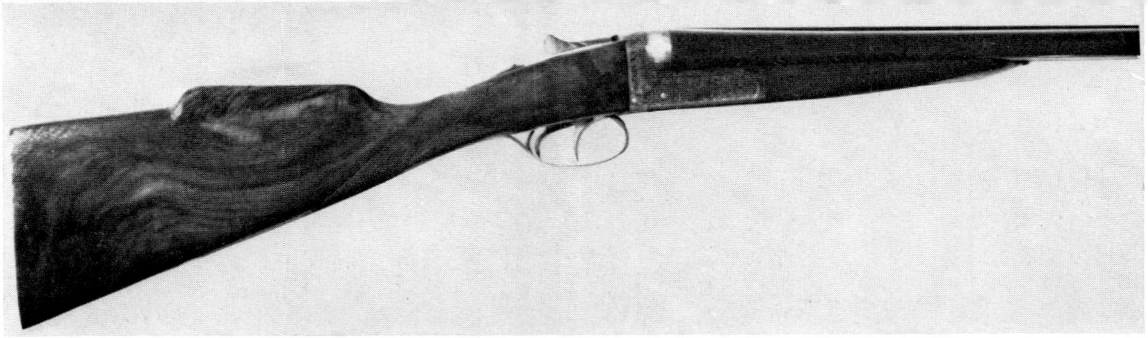

A comb raised to cure low shooting. The gun was correctly fitted to the shoulder, and the backsight (i.e. the shooter's eye) alone needed raising to restore accuracy

The Singlepoint sight as made for shotguns. The fluorescent Perspex light source is under the transparent dome on the right. The eye lens is on the left. The adjustments are for elevation and direction

Right : The French Darne gun in the open position. The fired cartridge has been selectively withdrawn with the breech and, when clear of the chamber, falls to the ground. See also the plate facing page 15

Below : A modern breech-loading punt gun by Messrs. Thomas Bland & Sons, with Snider-type breech action and spring recoil gear

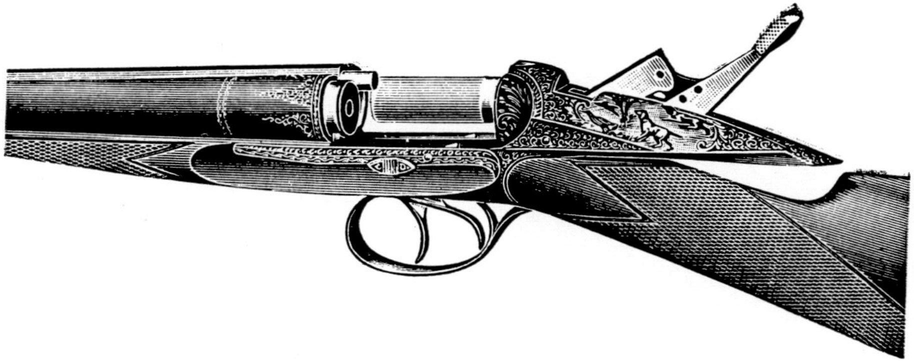

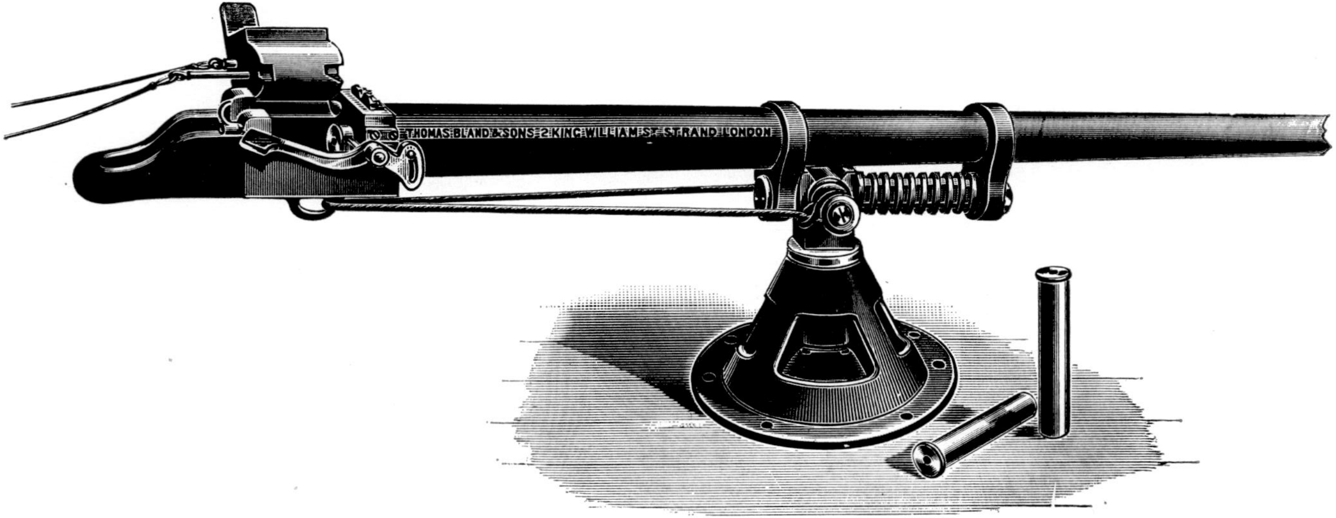

CHAPTER THIRTEEN

STOCKS AND FITTING

THERE is no doubt that the great majority of shooting men use guns for which they have never been properly fitted. They are guns which they inherited, or bought second-hand or ready-made. Sometimes the stocks have been shortened or lengthened to remedy a gross misfit; less frequently the bend or cast may have been altered, and by such adjustments the owner may occasionally have arrived at a good fitting. But in the majority of cases, the shooter is called on to adapt himself to a greater or lesser degree to his weapon. Thanks to the flexibility and infinite adaptability of the species, he usually succeeds in doing this sufficiently well to shoot satisfactorily, according to his natural ability, and without any significant discomfort.

Still, there can be no doubt of the added pleasure and proficiency to be derived from a really well-fitting gun—one that " fits like a glove ", and comes into place sweetly and easily, as though of its own accord, without obtruding itself in the slightest degree on the shooter's attention. To a man of normal physique, such a fitting is often attainable by minor alterations to an existing stock, and the requirements of such a fitting will well repay study.

First, we must be clear about our terminology. In this country, the dimensions of a gun-stock are normally defined by the measurements indicated in fig. 26 below, which also gives the names of the parts.

It will be seen that these measurements do not fully define the shape of the stock—for example, the depth from heel to toe, or the length of the comb measured forwards from the heel Nor is any note normally taken of the thickness of the stock, particularly as affecting the radius of the comb where it comes into contact with the shooter's face. These matters are usually left to established ideas of normality, though note may need to be taken of them in special cases.

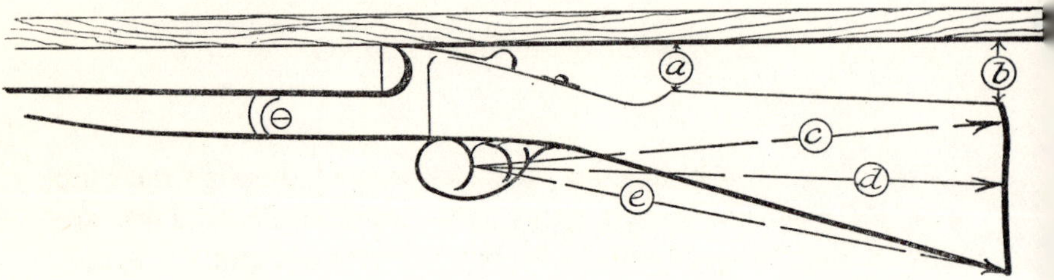

Fig. 26. The measurements of a gun-stock. *a* is the bend to comb, and *b* the bend to heel. *c* is the length to heel, *d* the length to butt, and *e* the length to toe. The lateral deviation of the stock, measured at the butt, is the " cast " : " cast-off " if it is to the right, and " cast on " if it is to the left.

Also, there is a dimension known to the Americans as " pitch ", to which they sometimes pay great attention. It is determined by the overall angle between the butt and the line of sight, but does not enter into English parlance. We avoid it by specifying the length of the stock at the three points shown.

Finding the correct stock. It is well known that if a man goes to two expert gunfitters he may collect two different prescriptions for a stock to suit him. Yet it may mean no more than that the two fitters concerned have different ideas of correct shooting posture. One, for example, may advise the shooter that he should face more towards the target than the other, and may prescribe more cast-off in consequence. Both fitters may therefore be right, subject to the shooter duly conforming to the advice given.

But there is something that overrides any such considerations. It is what I would call the principle of minimum adaptation, and leads to the conception of an ideal or natural stock.

Thus, it is agreed that the best results in wing-shooting are attained by instinctively pointing the gun where the shooter is looking, rather than by deliberate aiming. By use and habit, he may have become thoroughly accustomed to a particular gun and shooting posture, and may be able to shoot in this way with reasonable satisfaction and success. But if the gun requires any adaptation on his part—if he has to rely on doing this or that with his head or limbs or body—he will shoot well only so long as he does these things. They may indeed have become habitual, but under the stress of fatigue or excitement—especially excitement—such acquired habits can and do break down. When that happens, the thing that should be done to ensure proper adaptation may not get done, and the result is an incorrectly mounted gun and a miss.

The ideal is accordingly to leave the shooter free to take up what, for him, is a strictly natural, energetic pointing attitude, and to mould the gun, so to speak, to that attitude. It is the one from which he will have the least possible tendency to depart. What the attitude is may be found by experiment with any intelligent and uninhibited shooter, without a gun and preferably with no idea of the purpose of the experiment. He is asked to pretend to be pointing out something in the distance to a companion, using his left hand if he is right-handed, or *vice versa*. The thing, whatever it is, is fast disappearing, and it is vitally necessary that his companion, who is not so quick-sighted as he is, should be brought to see and recognise it. " Look!" he should say, " there it is—there, *there*!"

The result, with a suitable subject, is a delightful demonstration of the ideal shooting attitude—weight on left foot, left shoulder forward, head slightly forward and turned about 25 degrees to the right, and body turned about 45. If a gun could now be moulded to that attitude, it would conform to the principle of minimum adaptation: it would be that person's natural gunstock, not dependent on the acquisition of any special habits for correct mounting.

But the " moulding " would need to be correctly done. The butt must rest fully and fairly into the shoulder recess. The comb must rest snugly and firmly in the angle between the cheekbone and the jaw; and these conditions being satisfied, the eye must be in line with the rib and just above it. Bend and cast-off are thus determined. The stock must also be of the correct length—not long enough to catch whatever may be the appropriate clothing, and not so short that the thumb or fingers can strike the nose when the gun recoils. (I like to have a clearance of 1 inch between my nose and the tip of my little finger.) Too short a stock can cause or promote bruising of the second finger by the trigger guard. A normal length for an average man is $14\frac{3}{8}$ inches.

A vital measurement. A measurement of the utmost importance is the drop to that part of the comb which comes immediately below the cheekbone, because that is what determines the height of the gun's backsight, which is the shooter's eye. If the gun delivers its charge truly to the point of aim, the centre of the eye should come about $\frac{3}{16}$ inch above the standing breech. This will cause the gun to print its pattern about 6 inches high at 40 yards—a desirable thing in a game gun—and will normally require a bend to comb of about $1\frac{1}{2}$ inches. If the gun shoots low, the comb *must* be raised—say, to the extent of $\frac{1}{16}$ inch for every 2 or 3 inches by which it is required to raise the mean point of impact of the charge centre at 40 yards.

Low-shooting guns are commonly cured by straightening the whole of the stock. This is wrong if it raises the butt materially above its correct position in the shoulder. The vertical position of the butt (i.e. the bend to heel) should desirably be determined by the length of the shooter's neck and the slope of his shoulders, and by nothing else.

If the comb has thus to be raised to cure low shooting, it can be done temporarily and experimentally—or even permanently—by an indiarubber comb-raiser. These are procurable in various thicknesses from any good gunsmith and are stuck on the original comb with a modern adhesive. For a permanent alteration, a well-matched piece of wood can be added to the stock. If a man has an unusually long neck and sloping shoulders, he may require a bend to heel considerably more than the 2 to $2\frac{1}{4}$ inches found on average British guns. In that event, he may tend to suffer from bruised cheek—a condition that can be alleviated or cured by a level comb, or even one sloping slightly upwards to the rear.

American guns often have more bend than English ones, and no cast-off. A man accustomed to an English gun can usually shoot well with an American stock, but he has to adapt himself by leaning his head slightly over to the right in order to get his eye into line with the rib. This he can easily do by virtue of the greater bend; but his eyes are no longer strictly level, which cannot improve his shooting, and there is an obvious and regrettable departure involved from the minimum-adaptation principle which I think is so desirable to follow.

There are several minor aspects of gun fitting, but provided that a shooter has familiarised himself with the basic requirements here described, he will be in a position to pursue the complete satisfaction of his needs in his own way. A critical and observant friend can help to check the fit of an existing gun by noting any difference between the shooter's natural pointing attitude and his attitude when pointing the gun, particular attention being paid to the position of the head.

Variations. The normal two-triggered English gun has a straight " hand " or grip to facilitate manipulation of the rear trigger; but if a single trigger is used a pistol grip or, rather, a semi-pistol grip, has considerable attractions.

The normal English fore-end terminates just where most shooters prefer to hold their barrels. Some of the best gunmakers—Purdey's in particular—accordingly make the tip of the fore-end full and round, when it acts as a comfortable hand-stop, and tends to discourage changes in hold, which are not desirable.

The so-called beavertail fore-end, a broad and clumsy affair, is intended chiefly for the protection of the shooter's hand from hot barrels. Such a fore-end is a sad disfigurement to a good double gun, though a modified version, known as a semi-beavertail, can be pleasant to handle and is not too obtrusive.

Wood. The first requirement of a stock is that it shall be of sound, well-grown and well-seasoned walnut, free from shakes, galls and splits, and straight-grained through the hand or grip. A figured walnut stock is attractive in appearance, but can be less robust than one made of plainer timber, according to how the grain runs at critical points. But a stock so exotic that it cannot be taken into the field without causing its owner acute anxiety is simply a downright nuisance. There is little doubt that the average sportsman who is keen on a good gun pays more attention to the quality of his stock than he does to the quality of his patterns. Yet it is a great mistake to do so.

CHAPTER FOURTEEN

MISCELLANEA

Safety catches—Size of shot—Slugs—Trigger pulls Gun-cleaning—Ribs—Shotgun sights—Chromium plating of bores—Punt guns—The ideal battery

THERE ARE several aspects of the gun which, though of secondary importance, demand some mention, and in this chapter I hope to deal with most of them, though of necessity briefly.

Safety catches. The limitations of these devices cannot be too widely understood. In general, they merely bolt the triggers of the gun. They do not uncock the hammers or do anything to prevent them from falling and firing the cartridge if the normal means for holding them up should fail, as fail they may, and for a variety of reasons, Faulty construction or adjustment, undue wear, the intrusion of a particle of foreign matter, the swelling of woodwork, or even a simple jolt, are all capable of causing the inadvertent discharge of a gun at " Safe ". The only safe gun is an unloaded gun—not merely a gun that is *believed* to be unloaded, but one that can be *seen* to be unloaded. A conventional gun with dropped barrels may be considered to comply with this condition, even if it has cartridges in the breech.

Size of shot. This is the subject of never-ending controversy, in which a main factor—confidence—is frequently overlooked.

What keeps the controversy alive is that, within certain limits, there are compensatory factors at work which so nicely balance each other as to make the decision fairly one of personal choice and confidence.

But the limits must not be overstepped. The shot must be large enough to penetrate to a vital part, and the larger the bird the larger the shot must be to fulfil this condition. It is no use firing dust-shot at geese at normal ranges. On the other hand, the shot must be small enough to make a sufficiently close pattern, otherwise it becomes increasingly a matter of chance whether sufficient pellets will strike, however accurately the charge may have been centred on the target. Unduly large shot will certainly bring off some brilliant flukes, but, taking one shot with another, will not fill the game bag as well as will a more moderate size.

The popular sizes of shot represent the outcome of vast experience gained over centuries. The uncommitted shooter can safely adopt them and forget the subject. They appear to be as follows:

Partridge	6	Rabbit	5 or 6	Mallard	4
Grouse	6	Hare	4	Teal	5
Pheasant	5 or 6	Woodcock	7	Geese	1 or 3
Pigeon	5 or 6	Snipe	8	Squirrel	7

If, however, a man is quite confident that he does better with a different size, he would be well advised to stick to it for as long as his confidence lasts. Confidence in shooting is worth much more than marginal ballistics.

Slugs. Shotguns have, of course, been used time out of mind for firing single projectiles, ranging from solid ball (plain or patched) to the more modern Lethal, Rodda and Brenneke bullets. But none of these has enjoyed the popularity attained in recent years by the rifled slug. Indeed, in the U.S.A., guns specially adapted for firing the slug are now available, such as the Ithaca Model 37 "Deerslayer". This is a pump-action shotgun, bored true cylinder and fitted with rifle sights. Guns of this sort are acclaimed as the "poor man's deer rifle" and for deer shooting in close country are highly effective weapons in the larger calibres.

The appearance of the slug can be seen from fig. 27 except that it is deeply hollow, like a thimble. A 12-bore specimen when checked measured $\frac{3}{4}$ in. in length by about .685 in. in diameter. If undeformed, it would thus pass through the constriction of a full choke, which measures, say .689 in. When loaded in a standard game cartridge, such as a Grand Prix, this slug, which weighs 410 grains, give the following ballistics:

	Muzzle	25 yards	50 yards
Velocity (ft./sec.)	1,450	1,305	1,175
Energy (ft./lb.)	1,910	1,550	1,255
Drop (inches)	—	0.6	2.7

The muzzle energy is thus almost exactly the same as that of the .256 Mannlicher (1,960 ft./lb.), while the energy at 50

Fig. 27. 12-bore rifled slug.

yards rather exceeds that of the soft-nosed Mannlicher bullet at 200 yards. The knock-down effect of one of these big slugs, travelling with such energy, is formidable. Accuracy is not good from heavily choked barrels, but from a cylinder, 3½- or 4-inch groups at 50 yards may be expected.

The most likely sources of disappointment when using the slug are (1) firing at too long a range—50 yards is enough, and is a good range in wooded country—and (2) firing from a shotgun that has not been properly sighted in. This last operation is indispensable, particularly with a double gun. But the best prescription for a slug gun for woodland deer is undoubtedly a single-barrelled type, bored true cylinder, and fitted with a wide-aperture peep-sight adjusted for 50 yards.

Incidentally, a Firearm Certificate is needed to purchase slug cartridges.

Trigger pulls. There are two bad handicaps to good shooting that are insufficiently recognised. They are soft, dragging trigger pulls; and trigger pulls which, though clean and crisp, are of unfamiliar weight. The latter are the bane of the man who uses different guns from day to day. Even if he has had all his triggers regulated to the same nominal weight, residual differences are well capable of affecting his form.

The ideal trigger pull, as has often been said, should resemble the breaking of a glass rod. For an average man, a $3\frac{1}{2}$ to 4 lb. pull for the right trigger and 4 to $4\frac{1}{2}$ lb. for the left is about correct. With cheap guns I have met some surprisingly good trigger pulls; but I have also met some very bad ones—pulls that were not only soft, but exceptionally heavy, perhaps as much as 8 lb. Such guns should not be accepted. (See also Chapter 10)

Gun cleaning. I have preserved my guns in first-class order under the worst conditions obtaining in this country, including salt water and salt mud, with the following preparations only:

(1) Soapy water for removing salt and salt mud—hot for the metal work, and lukewarm, applied with a nail-brush, for the stock. (Never put oil on top of salt: never, that is to say, wipe a salt-contaminated gun with an oily rag until the salt has been *washed* off.)

(2) Young's 303 for the inside of the barrels only.

(3) Three-in-One oil for general lubrication, sparingly applied.

(4) Vaseline mixed with medicinal paraffin and applied with a camel-hair brush for protecting non-working inner surfaces.

(5) Boiled linseed oil plus one-third turpentine (both of "artist's" quality) for the stock.

My normal cleaning procedure after using corrosive cartridges was as follows:

(1) Remove visible powder residue by pushing through rolled balls of pre-cut 8-inch × 6-inch newspaper.

(2) Remove invisible residue and any leading with stiff, brass wire brush lubricated with Young's 303 and vigorously applied. (Turpentine helps if the leading is obstinate.)

(3) Wipe out with clean flannel patch.

(4) Apply Young's 303 with mop.

Nowadays, with non-corrosive cartridges, I merely skimp (2).

I always use a piece of flannel impregnated with Three-in-One for wiping the gun over externally.

After a thoroughly wet day, I remove the extractors and locks (or the bottom plate in the case of a box-lock); shake out all possible water and mop up any that can be seen with a clean cotton rag on a little stick and with cotton pipe cleaners. The locks themselves I put somewhere where they get nicely warm but not hot. I then put the remaining components, in their disassembled and ventilated state, in a warm dry place where they can dry overnight. In the morning I examine and re-oil them. I have never had any rusting trouble.

When cleaning a gun, the barrels should always be looked over for dents. These are best detected from outside. They should be raised at the first opportunity. A badly dented barrel should not, of course, be fired.

Incidentally, it is important that the turnscrew or screw-driver used for taking out gun screws should be accurately ground to fit the fine slots in the heads. The fact that it may be a proper gun turnscrew does not necessarily mean that it will fit.

Ribs. The value of ribs is another controversial subject. Many experienced sportsmen, and especially those most accustomed to driven game, insist that, in the act of shooting, they are completely unconscious of seeing their guns, and that therefore the rib cannot be of any significance as an aid to accurate performance. But though the barrels, and more particularly the rib, may not be consciously seen, they undoubtedly come into the shooter's field of vision, and by what he subconsciously but unavoidably perceives he may be aided and guided in the correct pointing of his weapon. In *Gough Thomas's Gun Book*, I have dealt with this matter at some length, but here I will only say that if a man *believes* that a certain kind of rib helps his shooting, then it *does* help, and he should certainly repeat it when ordering a new gun.

The trap-shooter, who seems to take something more resembling a deliberate aim, usually sets great store by his raised ventilated rib, partly as an aid to correct pointing and partly as a preventive or reducer of mirage, which, when a barrel is hot, can cause the rays of light coming from the target to be bowed downwards, as shown in fig. 28. The effect of this is that the target appears to be at *A* when it is actually at *B*.

Shotgun sights. Attempts have been made from time to time to improve the performance of the shotgun by various optical aids. The simplest are some modification of, or addition to, the familiar bead foresight. Clay pigeon shooters, for example, frequently favour an additional bead half-way down the rib. Luminous or semi-luminous foresights have also been tried, such as the Ithaca " Raybar ".

Ordinary low-powered telescopic sights have occasionally been used. A special application is that of a non-magnifying telescopic sight, which can be used with both eyes open, and has the effect of appearing to project a reticle or aiming mark to target distance.

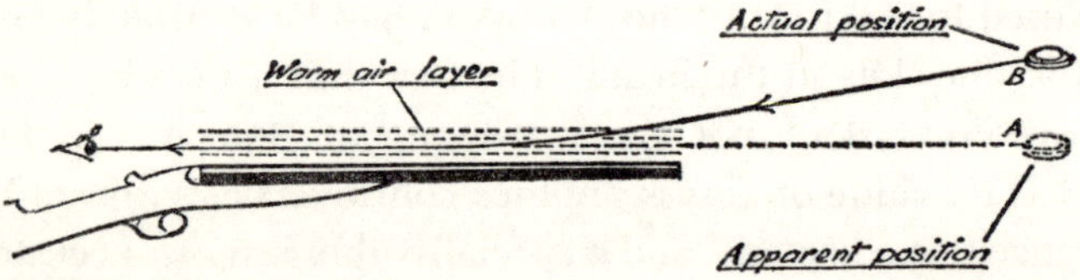

Fig. 28. Mirage created by warm air layer above heated gun barrel.

The American " Nydar " sight (no longer in production) was a variant of this idea. It, too, created an illusion of an aiming mark at target distance surrounded by a circle indicative of the extent of the spread of the shot charge. It could be used both for one-eyed and two-eyed shooting.

The " Singlepoint " sight recently developed in this country works on a different principle. In essence, it is a source of light arranged to project an image of a small spot of light *backwards* into what is normally the shooter's aiming eye. The other eye views the target in the ordinary way.

The effect is that the spot appears to be superimposed on the target, thus enabling shooting to be done in near-darkness if necessary. But this requires independent illumination, as by a radio-active light source. As currently made for use with a shotgun, the Singlepoint utilises the light from fluorescent Perspex, which needs daylight for its excitation.

The Singlepoint has the disadvantage of cutting off the view of the target to the aiming eye, but at the same time appears to be immune from parallactic error due to inaccurate gun mounting, whereby the eye is not located correctly in relation to the rib.

Chromium plating of bores. This process is much favoured by some foreign gunmakers, and is often made the subject of a sales story. But as a process capable of adding materially to the thickness of barrel walls without contributing to their strength, "chroming" is regarded with disfavour by the British proof authorities, who have ruled "that barrels treated in this way must be considered to have been potentially reduced in strength and be deemed to be unproved barrels under Section 110 of the Gun Barrel Proof Act". The buyer of a second-hand gun is thus protected against the possibility of serious pitting in the barrels being filled up and concealed by deposited metal.

As applied to new guns, chroming takes the form of "hard-chrome"—a coating of extreme hardness and microscopic thinness. It is claimed to protect the bores from corrosion, to eliminate wear, to reduce friction and thereby leading, and, by reducing the abrasion of the shot pellets, to improve patterns and to increase average pellet energy.

But, unfortunately, the kind of guns to which hard-chrome is most frequently applied are guns that have never had their shooting regulated at the time of manufacture, so that there can be no assurance that they give patterns of correct density or adequate quality. For satisfactory performance, such guns often need regulating, or at least the choke may need to be reduced. This can easily be done if the bores are left plain, but not if they are hard-chromed: the coating is so intensely hard that ordinary tools will not touch it, and some gunsmiths will not be bothered to work on barrels so treated. Chroming also complicates the commonest repair job—the raising of dents.

For the rest, when used with modern rustless cartridges, barrels do not need the protection of plating. Nor do they need any enhanced resistance to wear: with a bare minimum of attention they often improve with age and will normally outlast the shooter. As for the reduction of friction, leading and pellet abrasion, this is dependent on the bore being adequately polished before the plating is applied. Failing that, chroming may operate seriously and most obstinately in reverse. It is never applied to best English guns except to special order, and I can only regard it as being at best unnecessary, and at worst, a nuisance and a mistake.

Punt guns. The professional manufacture of punt guns in this country appears to have ceased. At the same time there is an undoubted revival of interest in punt gunning, and a number of amateurs with suitable resources have made their own. The more successful of these are generally constructed on the following principles.

The barrel is of seamless (solid drawn) steel tubing reinforced over the breech section by a larger solid drawn tube shrunk on. The trunnions are screwed and welded into this larger tube. The breech is a screw breech, and care is required to avoid unduly weakening the inner tube by the thread. The outer reinforcing tube should preferably be swaged and machined with an inwardly projecting shoulder to prevent the threaded portion of the inner tube coming back in the event of fracture.

Cartridges are paper cartridges crimped at the breech end and securely clamped between a solid brass head and a nut on a forward-projecting threaded portion. (If the breech has a right-hand thread, this thread should be left-handed.) The head of the cartridge can conveniently carry a dovetail for insertion in a corresponding recess in the breech face, whereby both are withdrawn together. The cartridge primer is a .32 revolver blank. The only powder used should be the large-grained, black, punt gun powder. The normal load for a punt gun is a pound of shot for every 100 pounds of gun, and 3 ounces of powder for every pound of shot.

The following weights, bores and recommended charges are taken with due acknowledgment from Stanley Duncan's *The Complete Wildfowler*:

TABLE 12

Punt Gun sizes and loads

Size of bore (inches)	Weight (pounds)	Length of barrel	Charge of shot (ounces)	Charge of powder (ounces)
1 - 1¼	50 - 75	6′ 8″ - 7′ 6″	8 - 12	1½ - 2½
1⅜ - 1½	80 - 120	7′ 9″ - 8′ 0″	16 - 20	3 - 3¾
1⅝ - 1¾	130 - 150	8′ 0″ - 8′ 6″	22 - 28	4 - 4¾
1⅞ - 1 15/16	160 - 170	8′ 9″ - 9′ 0″	30 - 34	5¼ - 6¼
2 - 2⅛	180 - 200	9′ 0″ - 9′ 6″	34 - 40	6¼ - 7½

The ideal battery. Wherever a high degree of manual skill has to be exercised, it is recognised that, for the best results, there must be total familiarity with any implement employed. This applies outstandingly to shooting; and although some shooters, more skilful and adaptable than others, may appear to shoot well with guns that differ considerably in several respects, there is little doubt that they would do even better if they could confine themselves to a single weapon. Accurate shooting depends on precise muscular response to visual stimuli, and the shooter who uses only one gun has deep channels of habit engraved in the nervous, mental and muscular machinery involved in the process. Give him a strange gun, and somewhere along the route a departure from the habitual channel of response will need to be established before he can use it proficiently.

So, for the best results of which a given man is capable, there is no doubt that the ideal battery is *one gun*—or a matched pair, or a single gun with alternative barrels, provided that they differ only in the matter of boring.

If, in order to cope with the different kinds of sport he pursues, a man cannot avoid having several guns, it is better, from the viewpoint of performance, that the guns should be conspicuously different as to weight, balance, etc. What is most prejudicial to proficiency is to have two or more guns, similar but by no means well matched, for the same class of sport, and to use them indiscriminately.

There are some riders to the one-gun philosophy. The gun should be a good one in which the shooter has complete confidence derived from undeniable experience. It should be well balanced, and should fit him to perfection. It should throw good and consistent patterns with the potentialities and limitations of which he is thoroughly familiar. Its mechanical functioning should be smooth and easy, and free from all sources of distraction. As previously emphasised, the trigger pulls should be crisp and of suitable weight.

The ideal gun (or pair of guns) should not be too new, or rare or precious. A regular sportsman could hardly be induced to appear with some of the beautifully chiselled and gold-bedizened specimens that one sees. Their place is obviously the show cabinet, not the field. So the ideal gun, to attain that state, has had its newness worn off. By honourable service, combined with good care, it has acquired a special patina—the unmistakable mark of a seasoned campaigner.

The sportsman who owns such a gun can afford to view with detachment, not to mention complacency, the array of beautiful specimens acquired by those more interested in collecting guns than in using them.

APPENDIX

Notes on Proof and Proof Marks

(1) Extracts from memoranda issued jointly by the British Proof Authorities

(a) *Information as to Barrel Enlargement—Details of Proof Sizes (Memorandum issued 3rd June, 1959)*

"Set out (below) are the nominal bore sizes under the 1954 Rules of Proof and the corresponding nominal figures under the earlier Rules of 1925:

BORE	*Rules of 1925* *OLD MARKING* *Nominal Size*	*Rules of 1954* *PRESENT MARKING* *Nominal Diameter*
12	12/1	0.740 in.
	12	0.729 in.
	13/1	0.719 in.
	13	0.710 in.
16	16/1	0.669 in.
	16	0.662 in.
	17/1	0.655 in.
	17	0.649 in.
	18	0.637 in.
20	19	0.626 in.
	20	0.615 in.
	21	0.605 in.
	22	0.596 in.

"At proof if a plug gauge of .729 in. diameter (but not one of .740 in.) will enter the bore to a depth of 9 in., that barrel is at present marked .729 in. and under the 1925 Rules of Proof would have been marked 12—and so on for the other bore sizes.

Rule 7 of Rules of Proof 1954 (as revised with effect from 1st September, 1966) reads as follows:

"If any Barrel of the First Class which shall be marked as proved under the Principal Act or these Rules, shall by any Process of Manufacture or by any other Means whatsoever other than the User and Wear and Tear thereof, be so enlarged in the bore that it will accept to a depth of 9 inches from its breech face, a plug gauge of the next larger diameter to that marked on the occasion of last proof or reproof, and thereby be unduly reduced in Substance or Strength, such Barrel shall be deemed unproved."

(b) *Black Powder Guns* (*Memorandum revised May,* 1960)

"A gun is proved for Black Powder only (and is almost certainly over 60 years old) unless the markings on the barrel include one or other of the following marks:

"Shooters are therefore urged most strongly not to buy any gun not bearing the marks of nitro-proof and not to permit the continued use of any such gun in their possession until it has passed nitro-proof."

(*New Eley Magnum Cartridges.* Note that normal English nitro-proof for 12-bore $2\frac{3}{4}$-inch and 3-inch chambered guns is not adequate for the corresponding new Eley Magnum cartridges, loaded with $1\frac{1}{2}$ and $1\frac{5}{8}$ oz. of shot respectively. These require guns to be submitted to a new Magnum proof; though the $2\frac{3}{4}$-inch Eley Magnum may safely be used in a 3-inch chambered gun proved to the normal nitro-proof standard.

Continental guns require to be proved to 900 kg./sq.cm. for the $2\frac{3}{4}$-inch Magnum cartridge and 1000 kg./sq.cm. for the 3-inch.)

(c) *The Repair of Gun Barrels by Welding* (*Memorandum issued 2nd February,* 1956)

"The Proof Authorities . . . warn members of the (gun) trade that the welding of any part of the barrel or barrels or the breech action body, breech-block or its equivalent is potentially dangerous."

(For the full text of these and other memoranda, and much other useful information on British and foreign proof and proof marks, see *Notes on the Proof of Shot Guns and other Small Arms,* issued under the joint authority of the Worshipful Company of Gunmakers of the City of London and The Guardians of the Birmingham Proof House—price 5s. 9d., and obtainable from either Proof House, at 48, Commercial Road, London, E.1, and at Banbury Street, Birmingham, 5, respectively.)

(2) Current Foreign Nitro-proof Marks

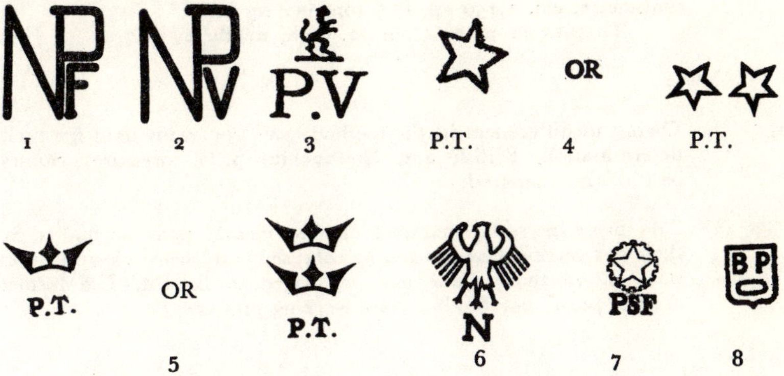

Key: 1. Austrian (Ferlach)
2. „ (Vienna)
3. Belgian
4. French (Paris)
5. French (St. Etienne)
6. W. German
7. Italian
8. Spanish

Two recently approved foreign marks are here shown to a larger scale:

9. Czech

10. Irish

(3) Metric Markings on Continental Guns

(a) *Bore and chamber length*: The nominal gauge followed by the chamber length in millimetres, e.g. 12/65 (12-bore, 2½ in.); 12/70 (12-bore, 2¾ in.); 12/75 (12-bore, 3 in.). Also the bore dimensions at breech and muzzle (but breech only on Belgian guns) e.g. 18.2/17.4 (.716 in./.685 in.).

(To convert millimetres into inches, divide by 25.4.)

(b) *Barrel weight*: The finished weight in kilogrammes, e.g. 1.42 kg. (3.13 lb.).

(To convert kilogrammes into pounds, multiply by 2.2.)

(c) *Proof pressure*: The nominal pressure in kilogrammes per square centimetre, e.g. 1,150 kg. (7.3 tons per sq. in.).

(To convert to tons per sq. inch, divide by 157.5.)

Notes:

(1) Owing to differences in the methods and apparatus used for their determination, British and Continental proof pressures cannot be directly compared.

(2) The proof pressures stamped on Continental guns or quoted in their test certificates must not be confused with the service pressures stamped on those made and/or proved in Britain. The former are test pressures: the latter are working pressures.)

INDEX

Actions:
- boxlock, 20
- self-opening, 24, 25
- sidelock, 20, 21
- sliding breech (Darne), 21
- trigger-plate, 21, 22

Adaptability, 35
Amberite, 94
American cartridge components, 87
Automatics (self-loaders):
- gas-operated, 28
- long-recoil, 26
- manually-operated, 26, 27
- recoil-operated, 27, 28
- short-recoil, 27
- weight of, 28

Balance, 32, 105-112
- a dynamic quality, 105-107
- data, 111
- definition of, 108, 109
- measuring, 109
- optimum, 112

Balling, 73
Barrels:
- aluminium alloy, 35
- chromed, 35
- fibre-glass, 35
- rifled for shot, 58, 59

Battery, The ideal, 127
Beauty, 36
Bolt-action, 26, 27, 32, 33
Bores, 18
- chromium plating of, 125, 126

Boss, 25, 34, 105
Box-lock, 20
Breechloaders, 71, 102
- pinfire, 16

Browning, F. N., 22, 27, 28, 32, 96
B.S.A., 34
Burrard, 17, 41, 46, 92, 93

Cap, 72
Cartridges, 70
- bad, effect of, 53, 54
- case:
  - functions of, 70, 71
  - length of, 72
  - types of, 70
- "Dispersante", 58
- Eley, 70
- imported, 81
- manufacture of, 74, 75
- "Maximum", 77
- new developments, 79-81
- spreader, 58
- "Wanda", 79, 80
- Winchester "compression-formed", 79

Chamberless gun, 80
Choice of gun—criteria, 31-38
Choke, 60
- automatic, 68
- best degree of, 66
- definitions of, 60, 61
- effect of, 61-63
- invention of, 63, 64
- recess, 60
- types of, 64
- variable, 35, 60, 67-69

"Winchoke", 69
Chromium plated bores, 125, 126
Clay pigeon guns, 97
borings, 98, 99
effect of expansion on, 100
MPI of, 99, 100
release triggers, 24, 25, 101
requirements, 97
testing of, 101
triggers and trigger pulls, 101
type of, 97, 98
Cleaning, 33, 122

Darne gun, 19, 21, 25, 32, 33, 34, 108, 111
Durability, 34

Ejectors, 22-24
Eley reloading notes, 87-91
Energy:
minimum striking, 41, 42
striking, 43
Evolution, a harsh, 36

Field, The, 64
Fire power, 35
Fitting, 113
Flintlock, 15, 16
Foreign guns, 37

Game charges, pellets in, 49
Greener, 45, 64, 32
Martini-action, 22
Greener, W. W., 64
Gun cleaning, 122, 123
Gun fitting, 113
Gun-rifle, 19
Guns:
choice of (performance), 39-51
choice of (type), 30-38
conventional, 19-25
boxlock, 20
hammer, 19, 20
over-and-under, 22
Paradox ball and shot, 22
self-opening, 24, 25
sidelock, 20, 21
single-barrelled, 22
sliding breech (Darne), 21
trigger-plate action, 21, 22
foreign, 37
modern, 18
repeaters, 26-28
bolt-action, 26, 27, 32, 33
gas-operated, 28
manually-operated, 26, 27
recoil-operated, 27, 28
weight of, 28, 29
second-hand, 38
Gun Trade Association, 37

Hammer gun, 19, 20
Historical background, 13
Holland & Holland, 25, 105
Home-loading and reloading, 82
black powder loads, 86
equipment, 83, 84
I.M.I. Notes on, 87-91
precautions, 83
procedure, 84, 85
recommended loads, 88, 89
Houiller, 71

I.M.I., 41

Kerné, 103

Lancaster, 25
Lefaucheux, 16, 71
Loads, 75-77
black powder, 86
high-velocity, 77-79
recommended, 88, 89

Magnum guns, 102
  small bore, 103, 104
Maintenance, ease of, 33
Manipulation, ease of, 32
Manton, 110, 111
Matchlock, 13, 14
Mirage, 123, 124
Miscellanea, 119-128
Muzzle-brake, 68
  principle of, 93

Newton, Isaac, 92
"Nydar" sight, 124

One-gun philosophy, 127, 128
Operation, quietness of, 33
Over-and-under, 22

Pape, W. R., 63
Paradox gun, 22
Patterns, 52-59
  close range, 58
  factors affecting, 54, 55
  minimum, 42
  percentage for all borings, 43, 62
  testing for, 55-59
Pellets in game charges, 49
Percussion muzzle-loader, 16
Pinfire, 71
Portability, 34
Powders, 72
  progressive, 76, 77
Proof and proof marks, Notes on, 129-132
Pulls, trigger, 121, 122
Punt guns, 126, 127
  construction of, 126
  sizes and loads, 127
Purdey, 105

Quietness of operation, 33

Range, 39-49
  maximum effective, 40, 41
  maximum killing, 39, 40
Reassembly, ease of, 33
Recoil, 32, 92
  brake, 93
  dynamic, 92, 93
  fallacy, 94, 95
  pathological cases, 96
  sensible, 92, 94
  velocity of, 93
Reliability, 34
Reloading, 82-91
Repairability, 34
Repeaters, 16, 17
  bolt-action, 26, 27, 32, 33
  gas-operated, 28
  manually-operated, 26, 27
  recoil-operated, 27, 28
  weight of, 28, 29
Ribs, 123, 124

Safety, 29, 32, 33
Safety catches, 119
Second-hand guns, 38
Self-loaders (see Automatics)
Self-opening actions, 24, 25
Shooter's Year Book, 41, 42
Shot, 73
  chilled, 73, 74
  cold-welding of, 74
  iron, 81
  manufacture of, 73, 74
  plated, 74
  sizes of, 119, 120
Sidelock, 20, 21
Sights, 124
  bead, 124
  luminous, 124
  "Nydar", 124
  "Raybar", 124
  "Singlepoint", 124, 125
  telescopic, 124
Single barrel, 22, 67

"Singlepoint" sight, 124, 125
Single triggers, 24
Skeet, 59
Sliding breech (Darne), 21
Slugs, rifled, 22, 120, 121
Spread, diameter of, 62
Stocks and fitting, 113
  gun measurements, 114
  the natural stock, 114-116
  variations, 117
  vital measurements, 115, 116
  wood, 117, 118
Striking energy, 43
Stringing, 41

Take-down, 33
Target, aiming, 67
Transportability, 34
Trigger plate action, 21, 22
Triggers:
  pulls of, 101, 121
  release, 24
  single, 24

Variable choke, 35

Wadding, 72, 73
"Wanda" cartridges, 79, 80
Weight, 28, 29, 32, 92
Weight and recoil, 92
Westley Richards, 25
Wheel-lock, 15
Wildfowlers, 49, 50
Winchester, 28
Winchester cartridge, 79
"Winchoke", 69